SUMMING IT UP

By the same author

Their Friends at Court
Irish at Law
Lost Causes
Poetic Justice
Law without Gravity
Vacation Business
Wills and Intestacies (with Robert Johnson)
Contract (with Robert Johnson)

Summing It Up

Memoirs of an Irishman
at Law in England

JAMES COMYN

THE ROUND HALL PRESS

This book was typeset
in 11 on 13pt Galliard by
Seton Music Graphics, Bantry for
The Round Hall Press Ltd,
Kill Lane, Blackrock, Co. Dublin, Ireland

British Library Cataloguing in Publication Data
Comyn, James 1921–
Summing it up : memoirs of
an Irishman at law in England.
1. Great Britain. Legal profession
I. Title
344.20092

ISBN 0-947686-67-3

Printed in Great Britain by
Billing & Sons Ltd, Worcester

For Anne, Rory and Kate

'I may be right, I may be wrong,
but I'm perfectly willing to swear . . .'

Opening lines of a well-known song,
taken by my pupil-master,
Edward Holroyd Pearce,
to describe a witness

Contents

Early Days

I WAS BORN AT BEAUFIELD HOUSE, Stillorgan, County Dublin, shortly before the tragic Irish civil war which followed the Anglo-Irish Treaty of 1921. Eamon de Valera, a survivor of the 1916 Rising, and the leader of the anti-treaty rebels, hid in remote, rambling Beaufield and its out-offices during the civil war. He and his faithful secretary, Kathleen O'Connell—there was nothing whatever roman tically between them—had been given refuge there by my mother and father, because Michael Comyn KC (my beloved uncle) was at the time, and for many years, principal legal adviser to de Valera and his party, and my father, a practising barrister of the Irish Bar and of the old Munster Circuit, was a subsidiary, minor, legal adviser of theirs.

I believe that my mother did not like being 'mixed up in politics' or in hostilities but gave de Valera a refuge and a welcome because her brother-in-law Michael Comyn, whom she 'adored' and who 'adored' her, had particularly requested it. De Valera remained hiding—successfully—in Beaufield off and on for some six months. He and his party duly lost the civil war to William Cosgrave and his provisional government of the 'Irish Free State', both militarily and at the polls and in parliament (the Dáil), but in the latter case quite narrowly. Eventually, ten years later (in 1932), de Valera and his party won power; and indeed his party have dominated Irish politics ever since.

It was a serious family misfortune that de Valera and Uncle Michael (then Senator Michael Comyn KC) 'fell out'—irreparably—just when Dev gained power, so that my uncle, and my father too, were passed over for legal promotion of any kind. Their legal practices suffered too, my father's particularly (it was then, sadly, the case that the law in all its aspects in Ireland was entirely influenced by politics, as indeed had been the case in England too). It was largely my father's disillusionment with politics which led him to send me away to school in England the following year—to the inspirationally chosen, delightful, Oratory School, founded by Cardinal Newman.

God gives you your parents—and you to them. I would not under any possible circumstances have chosen others; though, alas, I only very, very vaguely remember my mother, who died before I was two.

My father's family were an old north Clare family, the Comyns of Ballyvaughan, County Clare, which is at the edge of beautiful Galway Bay and at the foot of one of Nature's strangest, most fascinating, areas—the Burren; mile upon mile, acre upon acre, of huge solid limestone rocks; with very little vegetation (though making a good 'wintrage' for cattle) but world famous not only for its unique stone formations but for rare 'tropical' flowers and plants, and for rare wild life.

The Comyns of north Clare were, over the years, closely connected by marriage with many of the oldest Western families—the Quinns, the O'Loughlins, the McNamaras, etc. Grandfather Comyn and his wife (a Quinn) were evicted from the family farm-holding of many hundred years in 1879, together with their seven young children, by an absentee landlord, Lord Clanricarde, via his widely feared local agent, Joynt (an Irishman!). They were one of the many, many families thrown out on the side of the road, in the period 1840–90, by oppressive absentee landlords—because they could not find the ever-increasing rents. There were no agricultural or landlord and tenant or rent statutes in those days to give any form of protection or any form of court control.

Of the seven children three deserve special mention at this stage: my Aunt Delia, the eldest, was then aged just short of twelve (it was she who brought me up and bequeathed to me, on her death, my beloved Belvin, Tara, County Meath); Michael, then aged eleven, who won fame in after life, was the second child, the eldest son; and my father, James, the second youngest child, was two at the time of the eviction.

My father met my mother when he was a barrister on circuit on the old Munster Circuit. They met when he was at the County Clare Assizes at Ennis, the county town, having been introduced to each other by the redoubtable Uncle Michael, then beginning to make his mark at the Bar. He had become standing counsel to the Clare County Council and in that capacity he had come to be friendly with the vice-chairman of the county council, Peter Molony, an extensive and prosperous general retailer and wholesaler in Ennis. He had a daughter—Mary. Accordingly the Clare County Council 'match-made'!!!—and brought my father and mother together.

My father, like the whole family, was poor. My mother brought considerable money to the marriage (it eventually educated me, who never won a scholarship, exhibition or grant in his life). It greatly increased when, tragically, in four short years she lost father, mother, outstandingly brilliant eldest child Patrick (first place in Ireland in medicine) and brother John (a one-time novice in the Franciscan Order). Then very shortly afterwards, she herself died, together with the brother of mine to whom she had just given birth. Her 'fortune' was devoted to, and eventually fully exhausted upon, me. With my mother's dowry my father and she had bought a house in what I still regard as the loveliest city road in the world—Wellington Road, Dublin. This was No. 18. The houses there (they are, alas, now mostly 'converted' and many are offices) have lovely back and front gardens, each perhaps two hundred feet long and perhaps seventy feet wide.

My mother later persuaded my father that 'a country life' was preferable to an urban one. With his ancestry he

needed little persuading. They accordingly bought Beaufield beside the village of Stillorgan, some seven miles from
the city boundary. The house had twenty-four acres of
land, a considerable stretch of it being along the Bray
Road. Stillorgan is now a heavily populated suburb of
Dublin and Beaufield's acres (on which Kerry cows grazed
to provide the house with milk) are covered with hundreds of houses. The main house, only recently, suffered a
disastrous fire, but its out-offices remain, converted into a
magnificent, exclusive restaurant known as 'Beaufield Mews'
(with an antique shop above in what were the hay lofts),
owned and run by Mrs Cox, whose parents bought the
whole place—house, land and all—from my father in
1925. Beaufield's large walled garden (in which Dev used
to take the air at night) fortunately still remains too.

I 'gather in' now what to me are some rather interesting
things.

First, the Comyn family perforce had to leave Ballyvaughan—hurriedly—in 1879. But they retained, under a
sympathetic, more tolerant 'tenancy' just three fields (about
four acres in extent). After some 400 years of holding on
to them through a lot of thick and a little thin, they survived in the family and are now mine.

Secondly, in the 1820–40s Ireland had a population of
some eight million; Britain then had only some eighteen
million. Ireland's population was 'decimated' by famine,
plague and pestilence. The whole island now contains
hardly five million, whereas Britain's population exceeds
sixty million. Uncle Michael Comyn recalled a day at
Ballyvaughan shortly before the eviction when two boats
(they were commonly known as 'coffin ships' because so
many travellers in them did not survive) boarded over
1,500 people (more than one third the entire population
of the then impoverished Ballyvaughan district), bound on
emigration for the United States of America and Australia
respectively. I still hear, periodically, from descendants of

those surviving 'migrants'; people still very, very Irish in heart and sentiment.

Thirdly, part of my mother's inheritance was a house her father had bought in the Dublin suburb of Rathmines/ Rathgar for his children—principally Patrick, who was attending Dublin University (Trinity College). My mother and father unfortunately let it. Later they claimed it back—but failed to get possession because of a leading case, costly to them, recorded in the Landlord and Tenant Rent Restriction Acts books as *Comyn v. Leask*. I believe they wanted to go to the House of Lords about it!

Fourthly, my father some time after his marriage, bought at an auction in the Irish midlands for £2,000 or there-abouts (a very great deal of money then) two large solid bronze/brass horses with mounted persons and wings. Then and since known in the family (wrongly) as the Marley Horses, they were my proudest object possession until stolen from Tara in the Spring of 1990. My mother naturally asked about them on their arrival at Beaufield and merely said, 'James, what would your father say if he knew that you spent all that money on two horses which cannot even run?' Being what they are, they survived even the 1981 'bombing of Belvin', when the house was virtually destroyed.

I have a few, but vivid, memories of Beaufield up to the time we left it (when I was about five, my father sold it for some £5,000). He taught me a valuable lesson when he later said that he had no regrets about selling it: it had unhappy memories, and he needed the money at the time!

One memory is of a visit of a week or so from County Clare of my grandfather James Comyn. He had come up from the little farm where he lived with Uncle Pat (the son who remained at home to run the farm) and his wife Maria (Carroll) who looked after grandfather (The Gand, as I cherished him) until he died at the age of ninety. Grandfather Comyn was a highly educated, cultivated man. He had been in a seminary and was within months of being ordained a priest when he left to take over the running of the Ballyvaughan farm—from which he and his little family were subsequently evicted, as I have narrated. His elder brother had died and his parents urgently needed somebody to take his place. Grandfather soon afterwards married a highly capable Miss Quinn, whom I believe had been engaged to the brother who died. Grandfather was no good at farming, but his wife fortunately was, and then his son Patrick (Uncle Pat) took over.

In those days, leaving a seminary carried a social stigma; the person became known by the harsh and cruel description of 'a spoiled priest'. But apparently this was not the case when a young man left of family necessity, like my grandfather. It then, so I am told, was regarded as praiseworthy and not blameworthy.

My memory of Grandfather Comyn at Beaufield was of a delightful old man in dark clothes with a winged collar, actively interested in me—the only grandchild. We walked the fields together, examined the two Kerry cows (why has that excellent milk-producing breed been allowed to decline?), explored the woods, chatted to the donkey— my donkey—and spent a lot of time wandering through the rambling house and out-offices. His eldest child, Delia (Aunty D), was looking after me, having given up private nursing in England to do so. (Amongst many interesting things she told me was of seeing the *Titanic* set off on her maiden, and final voyage, amidst scenes of great celebration.)

I remember well the furniture in the house, because most of it followed us eventually to Belvin, and some survived the dreadful 'bombing of Belvin' of May 1981 and is in place in newly, identically re-built, Belvin.

I remember my donkey. I rode him to a show near the end of Beaufield's back avenue, beside Kilmacud church, and won first prize. This was not in fact a surprise, or a great attainment, because the class was for Black Male Donkeys, and though there were a lot of donkeys in the show, mine was the only Black Male Donkey. So was I introduced into the Show business of which I later became so fond.

I recall an occasion when there were extremely bright red lights at the back of a car which my father had just driven into the garage of Beaufield—at a point about where now the middle row of beautifully set candle-lit tables are. They belonged to a Hotchkiss car which he had just bought. Some years before, just about when he married in 1918, he was one of the first people in Dublin to own a car and drive it himself. It was, I believe, a Hotchkiss too, like the one I refer to. He had three or four of these lovely cars in succession. They were French, the product of the company which had made the famous Hotchkiss gun. They bore crossed-guns on the front of their radiators. They were rare in Ireland—I think in Britain too—but he used to buy them in London, drive them himself through England and Wales and have them shipped to Dublin. We are very far from being a mechanical family; but the cars were, happily, mechanically excellent. Their body-work and interiors were absolutely lovely. In the earlier ones, such as the one I saw on its first arrival at Beaufield, the spare tyre was mounted on the side running-board; as also was a can of petrol, which was usually the petrol called 'Pratts' or 'Ethyl'.

I also remember well the conservatory, or greenhouse, attached to Beaufield; a hideous thing, with hideous tall palm-trees and monkey-puzzles in it. By way of contrast there was the lovely walled garden, beautifully kept, with rows of vegetables, gooseberry bushes, raspberry canes, strawberries, ornamental bushes and little trees. There was an abundance of flowers. There were smooth, not gravel, paths between the rows, and a splendid path round the perimeter upon which I 'raced' a tiny bicycle. There were against the walls fruit trees, all labelled with names and events concerning their planting.

Beaufield was a very large, square, two-storey, cut-stone Victorian house, with about a dozen long, wide, stone steps leading up to the imposing hall-door. It was not very pretty. At the back it was really quite attractive; no longer absolutely square, for it had quite a few 'jut-outs', such as a sort of small round tower all the way up to roof height; and the back walls were not visibly stone or brick but were slated from top to bottom with what must have been large blue Bangor slates, interleaved.

We left Beaufield to go first to a house in Dublin owned by my nursing aunts, Lil and Mel (Mary Ellen), in Waterloo Road. It and its neighbouring, parallel road, Wellington Road, can be readily dated by their names. (Wellington was an Irishman, born in County Meath.)

It was soon afterwards that Aunty D, who brought me up, acquired Belvin, Tara, and we then had (and for some years enjoyed) the 'luxury' of a town house and a country house. Quite a turn-about in the fortunes of a family who had been evicted only about forty-eight years before (now of course one hundred and ten years ago).

I remember, from the age of five, the move from Beaufield to Waterloo Road. Two large pantechnicons (Anderson, Stanford and Ridgeway) loading the contents of Beaufield and unloading them an hour or so later at 15 Waterloo Road. It was a different firm (Strahans) who a few years later brought part of the furniture from Waterloo Road to Tara, about twenty-five miles away, and later brought the residue of it there.

Having Waterloo Road enabled me, first, to have a governess, then to go to the Sacred Heart Convent in Leeson Street, then to the Jesuit school, Belvedere College, and then across the water to England to the Oratory School near Reading.

Before we left Beaufield we lost our magnificent Kerry Blue dog. He had to be destroyed because he nailed the postman to the front door.

When I was at the Sacred Heart Convent it was the early days of the yo-yo and on one occasion, at Benediction, I was playing yo-yo with the thurible (censer) when the red-hot contents flew out on to the beautiful altar carpet. That cost my dear father well over £100.

Uncle Michael—Michael Comyn (1869–1953)

UNCLE MICHAEL—SENATOR/JUDGE Michael Comyn KC had a very great influence on my life from early on. He was a man who could exert influence. It was his example as an advocate and his obvious love of and facility for speech and language which led me from about the age of eight to want passionately to be a barrister. When one of my reports from school said, 'This boy talks too much', my father was inclined to be censorious, but Uncle Michael said, 'Splendid, he's cut out for the Bar', adding quickly, 'not of course that I would try to influence him in any way.'

My father and aunts would have preferred—often advocated 'a safer career', such as in a bank or the civil service. But, perhaps fortunately, safety—and pensions—do not generally speaking greatly attract the young.

Both Uncle Michael and my father would, I believe, if 'given their time again', have chosen the English Bar rather than the Irish Bar. I am certain of this with regard to my father; less so in regard to Uncle Michael, who was a man of remarkable foresight and could, I think, foresee that travelling would become much easier and quicker and it would be possible to practise at both bars. In the event I practised a little at the Irish Bar but mostly, very mostly, at the English Bar.

Michael greatly envied English barristers their 'barristers' clerks'. He got to know my Arthur and above all my Clement (Mulhern). They were at the head of their profession, and he studied with interest, amusement and pleasure how they attracted work for their chambers. Irish barristers did not have and still do not have either chambers (that is to say, a set of barristers together) or barristers' clerks. North and South, they operate from a law library. My father was interested in barristers' clerks for a rather special reason— that they fixed the fees with instructing solicitor and relieved the members of their chambers of all questions relating to remuneration. He found this particularly satisfying as he had always felt himself considerably embarrassed at having to bargain about his own fees with solicitors or their clerks— which is what those at the Irish Bar have to do.

I do not imagine Uncle Michael ever felt any embarrassment on this or indeed any aspect of practice at the Irish Bar. Knowing him he doubtless put a high value on his services—except when (as often the case) he gave them for nothing. This latter he did mostly in defending Republican prisoners before court martials in British days and again during the tragic civil war.

He advised de Valera and his colleagues for years on all manner of things. He defended Erskine Childers, who was shot while his appeal was pending; he appeared in court for Sean T. O'Kelly (later a leading member of de Valera's cabinet and afterwards President of Ireland), one such occasion being for 'contempt of court'. Among the others was in particular Mrs Kathleen Clarke, widow of the executed 1916 leader Tom Clarke (her brother was also executed). She was later lord mayor of Dublin. Both Uncle Michael and my father were very friendly with Mrs Kathleen Clarke and with her whole family, the Dalys, who ran a large and successful bakery in the city of Limerick, near the Sarsfield Bridge which crosses the Shannon into County Clare. They regularly visited the Dalys on going to and coming back from Clare, and of course during Quarter Sessions and Assizes. On one occasion of a visit to 'the Miss Dalys' at their bakery (they lived outside the city) I remember—with glee—that after a delightful tea my father and I emerged to find his lovely black Hotchkiss turned completely white— covered with flour!

Among many famous cases which Michael did as a KC was *Re Clifford and O'Sullivan*, which went to the House of Lords and is reported at 1921 Appeal Cases. It was a 'test case' in regard to forty-two men sentenced to death by a British court martial in County Cork. The case, though 'hurried along', gained valuable time for the men concerned; quite literally 'a stay of execution'. Although it was lost it was a real victory because the treaty came and saved and eventually released the men. Michael used to say that the case helped considerably towards peace because King George V came to hear of it and was properly disturbed at finding forty-two of 'his Irish subjects' under sentence of death.

Michael advised de Valera about many matters—Republican funds held by the Cosgrave government, Republican funds held in the United States, the formation of a political party (Fianna Fáil), the founding of a daily newspaper (the *Irish Press*), provisions for statutes, provisions for a constitution, constitutional questions and (among many other things) the land annuities. A few special words about the latter are appropriate because they affected the Ireland of my youth very greatly and caused what became known at that time, and is known in Irish history, as the 'Economic War'.

The land annuities were sums provided by the Anglo-Irish treaty of 1921 as payable by the Irish Free State to Britain as 'compensation' for land—usually estates of British people. Contemporaneously, or about contemporaneously, there was set up in the new Irish State the Land Commission, which parcelled out large estates to Irish farmers. These then came to be, in County Meath for example, Land Commission holdings, themselves carrying annuities, granted to small-holders from the West in return for their farms of far less quality in the West. These latter were in turn granted, as Land Commission holdings, either to people who had no land at all and wanted some, or to those who had farms which were too small to be economic.

When de Valera's party came to power in 1932 they were, as they had been in opposition and in arms, violently anti-treaty. They wanted to sever all ties with Britain. They regarded the treaty as of no true effect—as having been 'imposed' by Britain on Ireland. I merely remark quizically in passing that many treaties are 'imposed'. They are often 'leonine' but that is because one of the partners *is* a lion and enabled to claim 'the lion's share'.

Now, it appears that Dev, shortly before coming to power, received a formal opinion from Michael Comyn and George Gavan Duffy (later President of the High Court, but earlier a signatory of the treaty and earlier still a solicitor in England, the solicitor who acted for Roger Casement, instructing Sergeant Sullivan KC and Artemus Jones—of *Hulton v. Jones*—as counsel for Casement). Michael Comyn and Gavan Duffy apparently advised—and I respectfully believe quite wrongly—that the Irish Free State was entitled to withhold payment of the land annuities to Britain, presumably because the provision for them was imposed by something such as *force majeure*. This opinion Dev adopted, enthusiastically, and proceeded to implement when he came to power. Britain responded by imposing 'sanctions'—special tariffs on Irish goods. England was Ireland's principal market, especially for Ireland's principal product, cattle. The result was, I would have thought, inevitable. In the 'Economic War', Ireland could only come out the heavy loser, which is exactly what happened. I remember, young as I was, the difficulty my father and aunts encountered at Belvin about selling any cattle at all—fully grown bullocks changing hands at £4 to £5 and calves at a shilling or even less. I remember too seeing the cruel, self-destroying legend, 'Burn everything British except her coal.'

I of course was born almost contemporaneously with the treaty. I have no politics, and I think this is largely because I heard and saw so much of them when I was growing up. Apart from Uncle Michael being immersed in them, my

father was too. His attempt to gain a seat in the Senate—
when proposed by the Bar Council of Ireland—was
thwarted by politics, as was his strongly supported can-
ditature for the lord mayoralty of Dublin. He used to
emphasise to me that a brilliant barrister did not often
make a success in Parliament, or for that matter as a public
speaker or after-dinner speaker. The audiences and tech-
niques were so different. He recalled the Irish QC, MP at
Westminster who was howled down and remarked bitterly,
'And to think I am usually paid a hundred guineas for my
opinion.' Only one member of my chambers, averaging
twenty, ever entered politics. My master in the law, Edward
Holroyd Pearce, had no politics (he had no time for them
in either sense) but was a striking exception to what is said
above—he was a splendid after-dinner speaker. He used to
study his prospective audience, research both audience and
invitees, and plan his speech with care. He certainly did
not read from a script like one man he told me about did,
inserting every few paragraphs, 'Pause for applause.' Uncle
Michael was a good all-round speaker too—including in
the Senate.

Michael Comyn *was* a remarkable man. He was 'made' a
senator by Dev when he was in opposition. He tried for
chairmanship of the senate, was defeated by a casting vote
and became (*nem. con?*) vice-chairman. Then came the
falling-out. Dev later offered him a Circuit Court judge-
ship which he reluctantly accepted. It was on the Leinster
(Eastern) Circuit and he brought it to great prominence.

As a young man he had discovered gold, silver and phosphate deposits throughout the country and had obtained
mining rights for very small sums. With Robert Briscoe, a
prominent member of Dev's party, later the first and very
popular Jewish lord mayor of Dublin, he tried to mine
gold successfully in Wicklow. There *was* gold there; there
still is—in the Vale of Avoca (the Meeting of the Waters);
but it was wholly uneconomic. Our family got a few gold

rings out of it, and I believe that—grandly—Uncle Michael presented the Catholic and Church of Ireland archbishops of Dublin with altar ornaments of Wicklow gold.

Far, far different was the story of phosphate. In his native County Clare Michael opened some three phosphate mines, all within ten miles of his birthplace, eviction-place, Ballyvaughan. He employed quite a number of men. The mines were successful from the start. They became very successful when the 1939–45 war broke out, because it became impossible to get phosphate from North Africa, hitherto Ireland's principal source.

The Government, headed by de Valera—then on un-friendly terms with Michael Comyn—took over one of the mines compulsorily, under protest from him, and under further protest from him sought to pay him only a statutory 'compensation'. He sued them. In one of the longest cases ever fought in the Irish courts (forty-two days) he won all along the line, up to and in the Supreme Court. He was awarded damages, to be assessed by a judge. The sum turned out to be something like £30,000 (a very large amount at the time) but Government's other arm, the Revenue, took a toll. (He arranged a junior brief for me in his great case).

It was very satisfying for him to defeat Dev's govern-ment in the courts. 'My first case was a bad case and I did it badly. My last case was a good one and I did it well.'

He left a widow and two daughters—Marcella (Marcy) and Rose. Both are doctors (he did not encourage the Law for them), and to my pleasure Rose lives and practises within a mile of Belvin.

I think there is a hope of Rose's daughter Michelle coming into the Law—and bringing the family tradition from its present ninety-three years to over the century.

Keeley's Case

WE HAD A SORT OF FAMILY RETAINER, Michael Keeley from County Clare. He had served in the First World War with the Munster Fusiliers and came to my mother and father after the war and stayed with the family for the rest of his life.

Keeley claimed that his health had been badly affected by the war, in which he had served in several of those inexcusable battles which at great cost won or lost a few hundred yards. He considered that he was entitled to a war pension.

All his claims failed and he took his final appeal to a pensions tribunal due to sit at the Town Hall, Blackrock, County Dublin, a few miles from Beaufield, Stillorgan. Both my father and Uncle Michael offered to appear for him; both he politely declined.

He asked if he might borrow me, then about four and a half, for a day 'to keep him company'. Since he was often in charge of me there was thought to be no harm in this.

Keeley then proceeded to deck me out in my best clothes and we walked hand in hand to Blackrock Town Hall. After a little waiting the case of Keeley was called, and still holding me by the hand he went into the room where the hearing was to take place.

The tribunal consisted of three members. The chairman addressed me, in a friendly way. 'What's your name, young man?' 'James Comyn', I replied boldly. Apparently the chairman then knew who I was, because he was a barrister, a colleague of the law library of my father and uncle.

'And what brings you here today, little man?'

I drew myself up to my full height and said 'I've come to get Michael Keeley his pension. He thoroughly deserves it.'

All the members of the tribunal smiled.

Keeley got his pension.

He always said afterwards that I'd never do a case better (instructions are important in the law and one carries them out if one can).

The Oratory, Interviewed for Oxford, and an Irish Times Interlude

WHEN I ARRIVED AT THE ORATORY SCHOOL at the age of twelve, it was all very strange at first. I had never been out of Ireland, never away from home, before. Everyone in England seemed to speak a language which was *similar* to that which I had been brought up in but was at the same time very different; not at all so attractive.

The academic staff were good but not brilliant. We had an exceptionally good history master, Oliver Welch ('Ollie', of course), who subsequently went to Bradfield. To him I attribute almost entirely the interest I began to take in history, English and literature—good foundations for study at the law.

There was Mr Peacock, the science master, whose lab I nearly blew up and from which I was henceforth—to my delight—banished. I have a distant memory too, of Sergeant-Major Stanbridge, whom I nearly killed when I was first introduced to a .22 rifle in our galvanized rifle range. I can still on a clear night hear the ricochet of my bullets from galvanised-to-galvanised as I nearly, accidentally, killed off poor old Stanbridge. He was terrified of me ever after.

Henceforth I was—again delightedly—banned from the rifle range. It is, I suppose, one of the great arts of Life to get forbidden to do things one does not like. To avoid washing-up I recommend dropping valuable plates.

I naturally had many incidents while I was at the Oratory. My life seems to have been pleasantly interluded with particular incidents of one sort or another, mostly honestly unpremeditated and all, yes, all, well-intentioned, or nearly so. I once led the annual School Cross-Country for five miles over road, fields and ploughed fields and looked to be a 500–1 winner when I suddenly 'folded' on the Long Drive (the long Aintree-like run-in) and was passed by twenty-two of the other twenty-three runners. The twenty-fourth was unable to pass me because he broke his ankle on the Henley Road before the final straight. I expect excessive smoking of Sweet Afton cigarettes (which the village shop was good enough to stock specially for me) was the cause of this short-fall.

On one November 5th (it was called 'Bonfire Night', not 'Guy Fawkes Night', at the Oratory, a *Catholic* school) some of us decided to make a firework display outside the dormitories of a nearby famous girl's school, Queen Anne's, Caversham. They were friends of ours until then. (Happy relations resumed later, as witness my son Rory's Oratory School fixture list, which to my delight gave one fixture as 'Dance v. Queen Anne's, Caversham.' I like the 'v'.)

Seven of us went down to Queen Anne's with a variety of fireworks, and lined up at the edge of the playing field, faced in the direction of the main building and what we thought to be the dormitories. We let off our first cascade. Whereupon large and threatening men emerged from the darkness of Queen Anne's and ran towards us. We took to our heels. I ran across the middle of the playing fields in the general direction of the Oratory with all my might. I heard, or thought I heard, the padding of heavy feet behind me. Suddenly I was felled. I was temporarily stunned. An extraordinary thing then happened. I was wrapped up skilfully and completely in what I took to be a fisherman's net. I saw visions of being bundled, in a net, to expulsion and the Irish Mail, that hitherto welcome Express which headed home via Holyhead. As I suddenly came to, I found that in fact I had run full tilt into a hockey net and had become enmeshed in it. Happily there was no assailant, no pursuer, no sight or sound. Gathering myself and my senses together, I slowly made my way back to the Oratory, where I was happy to find my companions of the evening all tucked up in their dormitories.

Next morning the headmaster, then the Hon. Richard Hope (as yet unmarried to the matron) sent for nine of us; the culprit seven—and two others who were, on this occasion, completely innocent.

It soon appeared that intelligence between Queen Anne's and the Oratory must have been quite exceptionally good. It had identified the firework 'raiders' as Oratory boys (not too difficult, I suppose) but had got all seven culprits.

I was unfortunately at the end of the left side of the circle which formed before the headmaster in his study—and he started on the left.

'Did you, Comyn', he asked, 'participate' (I never cared for pompous words) 'in a so-called humorous episode at St Anne's School last night?'

'Yes, headmaster, I did.'

He knew better than to ask if I would disclose the names of the others. He asked the others instead. All admitted except the two who were innocent. He did not believe them until the rest of us (I think I was the leading advocate) persuaded him to the contrary. We were beaten by the headmaster; beating was rare at the Oratory. We were threatened with direr penalties (this often happened), and one of them, the stopping of 'leave out' for two or three weeks, was in fact carried out. 'Leave out' usually meant a trip to Reading to see a film—what was then known as 'going to the flicks'.

A curious incident occurred around the same time about a competition I entered for (I have since boyhood been a competition addict). Although my father and aunts were generous (their welcome cheques were, for a legal family, appropriately always in guineas), money was always scarce at the Oratory. We often resorted for currency to Mars bars—which could of course be halved, quartered or even eighted. I must have had ready money at the particular time, because I invested sixpence (a little less than half a modern 5p) by postal order, in a competition run by a national company to match two of their trade symbols out of about two hundred. Even at this length of time I had better not identify the company or hint too clearly at its identity. It continues, and so do its symbols. As learned opinions and judgments say, 'For reasons which will here-after appear' I will have nothing to do with its products and actively discourage others from buying them. One morning, about six weeks after entering this competition, I was summoned from class 'to see a visitor from London'. I knew nobody from London and was puzzled, but it was good to get out of class. I went to the main visitors' room and I found standing there a middle-aged pin-striped man. Everybody over twenty was 'middle-aged' to me at that time; in true retrospect I think he was about thirty. He did not have in his face the welcome that a visitor should have. I soon found out why.

'Are you James Comyn?'

'Yes, I am.'

'You are a school boy. You are not over twenty-one.'

I have always resented being spoken to in that way, and but for good manners (instilled by years of Father, aunts and Oratory) would have said, 'What business is that of yours?' I did in fact say something polite to that effect.

'You certified you were over twenty-one', he said, and produced from a small thin briefcase what I immediately recognised as my coupon.

'You were the only person to put in a correct solution', he went on, 'and I came here to present you with the £5,000 prize. But of course that cannot happen now.'

My immediate emotions were pleasure at having won and annoyance (bordering on anger) that I was apparently to be 'cheated' of my prize, on some absurd technicality.

'When we saw a school address', he said, 'we naturally assumed that you were a master, or a servant.'

I laughed at 'master' and 'servant.'

'It's no laughing matter.'

'I don't know', I said, 'why you should assume that a school address meant a teacher or servant. It would suggest to most people a schoolboy.'

He moved from being merely irritating and annoyed to being actively bad-tempered.

'In law', he said pompously (most people who begin like that are pompous), 'you are not entitled to the prize-money because the Competition expressly required entrants to state that they were over twenty-one, and you are not over twenty-one.'

I had smatterings of law even then. And I knew about equity (as much as I ever came to know about it). I tried to argue the matter. But my tribunal was hostile and had its mind made up (I have encountered that since).

He put the coupon back into the briefcase, snapped it close and took his little bowler hat and umbrella from the table and pranced out of the room. I decided not to go back to class but to have a consoling cigarette in the woods.

I told my housemaster, Ronnie Richings, about it later. I don't know why, because we never liked each other. He was neither sympathetic nor helpful. He said I had brought the school into disrepute and disgraced the house. I could not understand why—and said so. As so often happened in life, legal and lay, he gave a decision but no reasons. I, on the other hand, gave reasons as to why I was in fact a credit to both school and house and was the victim of injustice. Boys are very hot on justice. However, my appeals, and I, were dismissed.

I did not write home about the matter, but I told my father—and Uncle Michael—all about it when I got back to Ireland for the next holidays. Their reactions were predictable. My father was as always sympathetically understanding but quietly and gently pointed out that I was in the wrong and could do nothing about it. I always took things from him. Uncle Michael, on the other hand, was all for taking legal action. 'They wouldn't dare defend it', he said. 'Just think of counsel opening the case with the press and the country there.' I could well imagine him doing so, and given half a chance he would have acted for me. But my Father said No and that was that.

I missed the £5000—but I also rather regretted not even getting the sixpence entry fee back!

Interviewed for Oxford

At seventeen, everybody—the school, Oxford, my father—thought I was too young to go to Oxford, but I was determined to try, so that I could get to the Bar at the absolute minimum age of twenty-one. Accordingly, New College, Oxford, said they would consider me, but only after a special interview. This was in part due, I suspect, to my academic achievements not having been too good. I was sent to the interview equipped by my housemaster with a return ticket Reading–Oxford and thirty shillings for expenses, such as meals and buses at either end.

I spent about half the one pound fifty at Reading on cigarettes for myself and my friends. I was in good time for the interview, which was conducted by Warden H.A.L. Fisher (the historian), delightful Lord David Cecil and Mr Ogg (another historian, much more readable in my view than H.A.L. Fisher). They questioned me widely for about forty minutes. They seemed principally concerned about my age but could see, I think, my eagerness to start reading law. I was asked to withdraw. About ten minutes later the warden opened the door and said, 'Mr Comyn' (I was not accustomed to the title Mr), 'Mr Comyn—welcome to New College' and shook my hand. I was in!

I hurried off to send a telegram to my father, giving him the good news and determined then to have a really first-class tea. It was while having tea that I discovered I had lost the return half of my ticket and most of my money. I hurried back to the post office to see if I had left ticket and money there—but no.

Nonplussed and unable to get back to school, I suddenly thought of some foreign stamps in my wallet which a friend at school had given me. I searched out a stamp shop but they would only give me two shillings for them. I took it, on the basis that every little bit counted.

I then suddenly thought of my overcoat—one of Switzers' best. I enquired from a puzzled policeman where the nearest pawn shop was: 'I want to pawn my coat', I said, and he looked even more surprised. He kindly directed me, and it was not very far away. I went into the shop, took off my overcoat and asked how much. Little did they know that I would have to take whatever they cared to give. At first they offered £2.10s. but I bargained with them and eventually got £4. This enabled comfortable return to school and money in hand, of which I gave the housemaster nearly a half. He must have marvelled that I of all people should have money over.

I had difficulties about the missing overcoat when next home in Ireland. I never redeemed the coat. I was not in Oxford for several months and by then had lost the pawnticket.

I think there is a certain novelty about my first experience of Oxford University.

Six Months with the Irish Times

I had just short of six months to fill in between leaving the Oratory School (with great sadness) and entering New College, Oxford, in the Michaelmas term. I had thought simply of Belvin, family, farming, planting some new trees (a life-time hobby of mine), writing light verse and short stories, and some golf. With regard to the latter I loved

the game but was not good at it; the best I ever achieved
was a handicap of fourteen; it has now risen a good deal.
At the last English Bar golf tournament which I attended,
that old chum of mine, Mr Justice Michael Davies, faithful
friend and admirer of my golf, had £5 each way on me at
the 100–1 which Richard Hartley QC ridiculously offered
against me winning the matchplay; quarter odds the place.
It turned out to be a pretty close run thing; I got into the
last sixteen but, alas, no further. How many were there
entered, you ask? Please do not ask. It was incidentally
Michael Davies who bought a painting of mine, of mountains in Connemara—I only paint mountains—at the
Lawyers' Exhibition in Lincoln's Inn a few years ago, at
the asking price of £25. He need not have said to me afterwards that the frame alone was worth £20.

Idling or oodling the near six months before entering
Oxford was not my father's idea for a seventeen-year-old.
He had an old friend, the great editor R. M. Smyllie, of that
great newspaper, the *Irish Times*, in my view, one of the
world's great newspapers. Editor Smyllie would employ me
as an odds and endser at £2.10s.0d. (£2.50) a week, rising
to perhaps £2.15s.0d., and even £3, depending on progress.
He'd get me a temporary NUJ card. I accepted gratefully.
I started the following Monday.

It was a delightful six months for me. What was it, then,
that prompted the Great Man to say, on parting with me
in September 1938, 'God knows how you'll eventually turn
out, Comyn. But what have I done to have had inflicted
on me first Patrick Campbell and then you? Your poor
dear father, God help him. He has to put up with you the
whole time. He's a very decent man—as I now know; a
very long-suffering man.'

Well, things had been a little eventful. I was first made
stand-in film critic, with about fifteen films a week to see,
plus the Theatre Royal in Hawkins Street, where they ran
a three-part show—film, electric organ and impeccably
evening-dressed Jimmy Campbell with a full orchestra and

the lovely looking 'Royalettes'. I had to provide about a quarter of a page twice a week.

It took a bit of doing to fit in about fifteen films a week, especially when I used to sit the Theatre Royal show two or three times round. I got two complimentary tickets for each cinema and for the Theatre Royal. I had no girl friend. My friend since childhood, Patrick Reeves-Smyth, whose family firm of sack merchants was only twenty-five yards to or so away from the Theatre Royal, used to accompany me there but not elsewhere; and he had to be at school, at Downside, part of the time. Otherwise I attended alone.

All went well at first. I vividly remember—and have pasted in a scrap book before me as I write—my first 'article', or rather series of paragraphs; and my first mention in a cinema theatre advertisement ('Excellent entertainment—*I. Times*') in a Theatre Royal advert. Nothing very inspiring, nothing very original, in that, you may say. Alright—but the words *were* my own and they were used in the advertisement.

After about three months things went wrong—in a big way. I reviewed a film which I had 'slept through'—and I criticized it. I got the basic facts wrong; the main character was *not a* Catholic priest, as I sleepily assumed and wrote, but an Anglican vicar. No wonder I said, 'They should have done their home-work properly about Catholic priests. There were several bad mistakes in the portrayal of the leading character, a Catholic priest.' That went in the paper. Next morning at about 11 a.m. Mr Smyllie shot open a little hatch-door which divided him from the small but crowded 'news room' in Westmoreland Street where I was having a pleasant morning coffee with a nice Mr Alec Newman (later to be editor) and others, who included another kindly man, Mr Alan Montgomery.

The Great Man, the Great Voice, bellowed, 'Comyn , Comyn.'

I leapt to my feet and shouted (you had to shout to be heard through the hatch-way), 'Yes, sir, Yes, Editor.'

'Comyn, Comyn here straight away.' He liked that pun, which was no new one to me.

I came in pronto. Mr Smyllie was on his feet, in a rage.

'Comyn, you have in three and a half months managed to ruin this great newspaper.'

'What *have* I done, sir?'

'You have cocked up a film review. That's what you've done. I've had messages from Bloody Metro, Bloody Goldwyn and Bloody Mayer. And from their solicitors in Dublin and London. There'll be writs. And I'm delighted to say you'll be sued too.' Then, as an afterthought, 'Are you old enough to be sued? I hope you are.'

He raged for about ten minutes—and could he rage! He *commanded* me to write a cringing, crawling, apology for next day's paper and to have it published over my own name, not signed just 'film critic'.

'That's for starters', he said. 'Come back to me when you've written it and show it to me. We don't want any mistakes *in the Apology*. I've heard of newspapers, English newspapers, going down for thousands of pounds for *that*. As it is, you'll probably cost us £2,000, and we just can't afford it.' This was £2,000 in 1938 money. In sterling.

I stumbled out of the editor's office, and with the help of nice Mr Newman and my other new-found friends I wrote a short, abject, but dignified 'correction', typed it, checked it and, clutching it firmly, knocked on the editor's door.

'Come in, Comyn', roared the Voice.

I proffered the 'correction'. He read it quickly.

'Correction be damned', he said. 'This has got to be headed "Apology".' He took up an enormous red pencil, boldly struck out the heading 'Correction' and, in large lettering, put in the word 'Apology'.

'Will that be all, sir?' I asked, mouse-like, as I took back the 'Apology' which he threw at me otherwise unaltered.

'No, it will not', he shouted. 'You're fired. In spite of being your father's son, and I'm fond of your father, you're fired. God help your poor dear father. Collect your money downstairs and get out of here, get out quickly.'

I was very distressed, I showed it. As I got near the door he suddenly said, in a much quieter voice, 'No, I've acted hastily. Other people have made mistakes and I haven't fired them.' I knew that to be true. About sixteen months previously his masterpiece of a leader on 'The Abdication' had gone out, in the British edition (!) printed upside down! Apparently all Westmoreland Street had reverberated with his elephantine frenzy, but eventually he had laughed, saying something to the effect that it was a bloody good leader even if printed upside down—a bloody sight better than the leaders in those bloody English papers, printed right way up. And everybody concerned was quickly forgiven.

'Tell you what I'll do', he said, actually putting a friendly hand on my shoulder. 'Make you assistant racing correspondent for six weeks and see how you get on. Introduce yourself to Napley' (I think that was the name) 'if you can find him; he's probably drinking at The Bailey. Apart from drink he's a good chap. Tell him I've said you're to be his Assistant for six weeks. But you're not to have a single thing of yours printed without him passing it first. Same pay, though I should reduce it. Now, behave yourself.'

'Yes, sir', I said gratefully.

I found Napley, or whatever his name was. A very pleasant man, dressed in loud checks and wearing heavy brown brogue shoes—with spats. He had a very loud tie. We liked each other at first sight. We had a splendid time together. We went to race meetings together. I phoned back reports by him from the Curragh or Phoenix Park or Leopardstown (bars) to head office. I ran 'messenger' for him. I checked references. I was useful, because I already knew something about racing, National Hunt and Flat.

My dear father, to whom I of course confessed and told all, was pleased that I had not been sacked ('You deserved

to be, you know. Bloody silly thing you did'), but was
slightly apprehensive about me getting officially mixed up
in racing. He knew of course that I betted. I had for years
betted at the Oratory—on anything; in Mars bars mostly;
in money (a shilling each way via a groundsman) when I
had it to spare (after birthday cheques, etc.). My father and
aunts were generous with little cheques. They could not
afford much. Despite my mother's money (set aside for my
education), we were running low, and were to run lower.

All went well at the 'Racing Desk' (two stools at The
Bailey mainly). Mr Napley, if that was his name, even let
me give a tip or two. One actually came up, at a big price.
But the Editor didn't much like my idea for a little piece
headed 'A Sporting Oxford Treble'—£1 Win Treble: Oxford
for the Varsity Cricket Match in June, Oxford for the Varsity
Rugger Match next December, Oxford for the Boat Race
in Spring'. Napley liked the idea, 'except', he said, 'it's a
bit too spread out in point of time.' It was never used.
'Spiked' is, I believe, the technical expression. Then I was
transferred to three weeks or so 'on the streets', from which
I think I contributed absolutely nothing to the Great Paper.

Then (I must have done something wrong) I was moved
to 'Advance Obituaries', of which I had never heard before.
Working alone and unsupervised again, I was to dig out
the obituaries file (which was enormously big in width and
depth). I was to bring up to date existing advance obituaries (which were designed to go into the paper quickly
with the bare minimum of alteration) and to write new
ones about prominent people, Irish, British and World,
who had not up to then any ready-made entry. 'Put in
plenty of politicans', Mr Smyllie said, 'but include Religious
people and, if you like, sportsmen; you ought to be good
about sportsmen—sportsmen cut off in their prime, remember.' I had a happy and interesting month doing that. It
was fun and I was my own master. Noboby seemed to
check, even care about, what I was doing. I occasionally
consulted with Mr Newman. He was always helpful.

I had by now a good many friends in the news room of the *Irish Times.* I was learning a great deal from them. A silly memory: 'Thus' was 'an academic word', never to be used. (The BBC later didn't like academic words either.)

Mr Newman remained my best friend. I would miss him when in three weeks time or so I left to prepare for Oxford. I would like to work for the *Irish Times* in vacation, but I thought I would hardly be taken on again unless Mr Newman became editor or assistant editor.

My pay had been increased to £2.17s. 6d. a week. The return bus fare from Dublin to Tara was only 1s.6d. a day (the return is now over £3). My father used to meet me at the bus whatever the time, whatever the weather.

I heard some very good stories. Especially Patrick Campbell stories. I never met him, unfortunately. He had gone—voluntarily—quite a time before I joined.

The one I liked best was about Mr Smyllie, after the paper had 'gone to bed', entertaining top men of his at The Bailey. Patrick Campbell came in. 'Ah, I see you have your wits about you, Editor'. Mr Smyllie eyed him coldly. 'I'd need my wits about me with you around, Campbell.' It must have been one of the periods when—as happened to me—Patrick Campbell earned a black mark.

Another concerned P. C. being sent to Paris for the paper to cover something special. He did it unexpectedly quickly and of course well. He then sent a telegram to Mr Smyllie, from the George Cinq Hotel saying: EDITOR, IRISH TIMES, DUBLIN. NEED A REST. WILL RETURN TO JOB NEXT MONDAY. PATRICK CAMPBELL. Ten hours later he got a reply: WHAT JOB?, SMYLLIE, EDITOR, IRISH TIMES.

I heard a nice story about Oliver St John Gogarty (the famous Dublin surgeon, author, poet, wit, aviator etc., friend of the great Irish Literary Revival set, author of *As I Went Down Sackville Street* and *Tumbling in the Hay.*) On entering a bar off Grafton Street, he saw James Joyce in a corner, with a patch over one eye, sipping a Guinness alone. 'Ah, Joyce', said Gogarty boisterously, 'drink to me only with thine eye.' I believe it was Patrick Campbell who told Gogarty that 'there is one law for the rich and half a dozen for the bloody poor.' And the story of the three doctors of eighty-five walking in Stephen's Green has the touch of Campbell about it. It was Spring and the aged doctors saw a pretty girl in a lovely dress. 'Ah,' said one, 'if only I were eighty again!'

Mr Newman used to muse what sort of report Joyce got in English when with the Jesuits at Clongowes Wood. 'I expect', he said, 'it went something like this: "This boy shows aptitude in this subject but will insist, tiresomely, on inventing words of his own" !'

Alfie Byrne, a publican, was the most popular man in Dublin—seventeen times lord mayor. Apparently he was not generous about drinks in his pub. On one memorable occasion, the pub was not very full, but contained many of the literati. Suddenly Alfie Byrne said, 'Drinks on the house!' 'Good God', said Sean O'Casey, 'as the critics say, it brought the house down.'

I liked the story about Alfie Byrne, ever on the look out for votes, always saying to people, particularly children, when shaking their hands, 'And when you go home tell them you've shaken hands with the great Alfie Byrne, Lord Mayor of Dublin.' On one occasion he practised this when visiting Dundrum Criminal Lunatic Asylum. Shaking hands with a morose individual who was sitting alone in a corner, he said, 'Tell your relations and friends you've shaken hands with Alfie Byrne, the great Lord Mayor of Dublin'. The old man shook his head sadly. 'Poor man,' he said; 'when I first came in here I thought I was Michael Collins. They'll knock that sort of nonsense out of you within a week.'

The nice staff of the *Irish Times* recalled for me one of the few libel actions which I was told that great newspaper had been involved in. Side by side on the front page it had printed two stories. One about a man's appeal to the Court of Criminal Appeal. The other about a dreadful accident to a man who had fallen off a ladder doing some repair work at the Mater Hospital in Dublin. Most unfortunately the last paragraph about the wholly unsuccessful, unmeritorious appellant got put in as thc last paragraph about the man who had fallen off the ladder. It said, quoting the Chief Justice in the CCA case, 'Moreover, he has seven previous convictions, mostly for violence'! The *Irish Times* settled the action quickly but it cost them a couple of thousand pounds. (Nobody ever sued us about my ghastly film review, I'm glad to say. 'Bloody Metro, Bloody Goldwyn and Bloody Mayer' graciously accepted my apology.)

Back to 'Advance Obituaries'. Apparently the editor himself, in an idle moment, had called for the file and had flipped through it to see what young Comyn had been doing. Most was OK, but he came across an item where mischief had entered into me. It was headed, say, CARDINAL MILANO. It was an updating entry, not new one. I had written in, quite properly. 'He was one of the oldest cardinals when he died, aged . . . . He had achieved the greatest honours Rome could give. He had become etc., etc.' So far so good. But then, terribly (I agree), but as a touch of badly-needed well-intentioned 'humour', I had added, off my own bat, 'His Eminence was unmarried.'

I had written that some days previously. Then one morning during my last week with the great newspaper, Mr Smyllie threw open his hatch and bellowed, like a wounded elephant, 'Comyn'.

I went in.

He threw the offending Advance Obituary on the table.

'Just think', he said in measured tones, 'if that Cardinal had died at 11 p.m. last night, we'd have slotted this into the news quickly. And we'd have been ruined. And made the laughing stock of the world. Oh, Comyn, words fail me.' They never did.

He calmed down and said, 'You're leaving us at the end of this week, thank God.' And then the words I have mentioned at the start: 'God knows how you'll ever turn out, Comyn. . .'.

He relented, as always, a little later. He advanced my departure by a couple of days, gave me a tiny 'copper hand-shake' and wished me luck. Unfortunately, I never saw him again. He suffered badly from diabetes and died com-paratively young. He used to bicycle everywhere. He lived, I think, at Delgany. I wonder if he bicycled back there at night.

He was a Very Great Man. The *Irish Times* was then, and now is, a Very Great Newspaper.

As a matter of fact, I *have* written for it since. In fascin-ating weekly competitions which it runs. I enter in bouts.

Oxford

I was thrilled to be reading law at last and found all sub-jects interesting apart from real property, which in England is of course based on the 1925 laws. I found it dull and difficult. Eventually I got a second class and then converted my BA into an MA, which one can at Oxford simply by payment—just like converting a try at rugger.

At the same time as studying for law finals at Oxford, I studied for Bar finals, which though covering the same ground call for short factual answers to questions rather than the essay type of answer required at Oxford. I joined the Inner Temple and passed Bar finals while at Oxford. Taking Bar finals in London I spent three nights at the Strand Palace Hotel at 10s. 6d. (52½p) bed and breakfast per night

At Oxford I spent a lot of time at the Oxford Union, the world-famous debating society. Eventually I became Presi-dent of the Oxford Union—one of very few Irishmen and the second old Oratory boy (the first was Hilaire Belloc).

I became president by beating Roy Jenkins (now Lord Jenkins and chancellor of the university), by four votes after many recounts. At the presidential debate the night before, he had as his guest speaker quite the best orator I have ever heard, Nye Bevan, Aneurin Bevan.

I also became president of the Oxford Newman Society, which was very suitable and very gratifying for an Oratory boy. Oxford always meant a great deal to Newman.

I played squash for the university, alternating as fifth string with a friend, Tony Roper. To get a blue it is necessary to play against Cambridge and he deservedly got his place against Cambridge. The captain had asked us to play three matches against each other to decide the fifth place and Tony Roper beat me 2–1. He then went on to win the match against Cambridge.

Close friends of mine at Oxford were J.A.T. Douglas and his fiancée Mary. I was their best man. Jim became a high official of Conservative Central Office and Mary has become one fo the world's greatest authorities on anthropology.

5

Mr de Valera Sends for Me

PROBABLY THE MOST astonishing experience I have ever had was to receive quite out of the blue when I was at Oxford a letter from Mr Eamon de Valera, then taoiseach (prime minister) of Ireland, at the end of Easter term 1939, asking me to come to tea with him.

Some Dev documents survived the Belvin fire but not that letter. However, I remember it clearly. It was addressed to me at New College. It was almost word for word as follows: 'Dear James, I have not seen you since you were a baby at Beaufield with your dear mother. I would very much like to see you again. Your Term is now ending and no doubt you will be returning to Ireland during the next few days. If Wednesday or Thursday of next week would suit you to come and have tea with my wife and me, would you let my secretary know and I will arrange for a chauffeur to meet you wherever you suggest. Yours sincerely, Eamon de Valera.'

It is to me typical of the man's thoroughness and skilfulness that he should have known where to find me and at a precisely suitable time. It was also interesting that he did not suggest collecting me at Belvin, where my father lived.

I felt that I could not tell the family about the letter. I also felt that the invitation was one which I must accept. I accordingly telephoned to his secretary, fixed a day and said that there was no need for anybody to meet me and that I would present myself at the taoiseach's office at Government Buildings shortly after 3 p.m. Without telling the family precisely where I was going I departed from

Belvin for Dublin for the day. At the taoiseach's office I
received a friendly greeting from his secretary and was only
kept a few minutes before being ushered into the Great
Man. Everyone knew him as The Chief. I could not help
thinking that Michael Collins ('The Big Fella') had very
aptly called him 'The Long Fella'. He was tall, thin and
already then nearly blind, wearing very strong spectacles.
He had a ready, if rather wintry, smile and gave me a great
welcome.

He brought me by car to his private house in Booters-
town Avenue, off Merrion Road, Blackrock, where I met
his delightful wife, a small, shawled old lady who looked
like a delicate piece of china. She talked to me about her
great interest, Irish fairy stories and folklore, on which she
has written delightful books.

I was nearly three hours in Dev's company and they are
amongst the most interesting I have ever spent. He mentioned my mother frequently and with great affection. He
said she was one of the most charming ladies he had ever
met and that he owed her a lot. But from first to last he
made no mention of any kind of either Uncle Michael or
my father.

He appeared to know everything about me and I soon
found that a purpose of the invitation, probably *the* purpose of it, was skilfully and fully to interrogate me about
the views and attitudes of the young men at Oxford. He
also interrogated me about my own views on international
and Irish affairs and about my own plans for the future.
'Interrogate' is the right word, for he kept up a barrage of
testing and searching questions.

What seemed to me, from my experience in England
and Oxford, the likelihood of war? And how would the
youth of England react to war? Was not that notorious
Oxford Union motion that they would not fight for King
and Country misleading, and when it came to the point
they *would* fight? On that he had a correct view when the
Dictators had a superficial and misleading one. Indeed he

was remarkably well informed on everything he asked me about.

He was very interested to know the English undergraduate view about Ireland—its partition and the neutrality the Twenty-Six Counties would maintain in the event of war. I told him, as he obviously anticipated, that Irish neutrality would be greatly resented in England. Would it be respected? I said that I thought it would be by the English, unless the Germans threatened it or abused it. He even asked me how likely I thought that would be. He appeared to think it likely that Germany would attempt to invade Ireland and that she would then perforce be allied to England. And in that he seemed to see the end of partition.

As to Irish neutrality he was adamant, saying that the people would want it and, if the Twenty-Six Counties threw in their hand with England, in the first place they would suffer considerable damage from the Germans and probably become a battleground.

He was very interesting in his forecasts—upon which he quizzed me. He thought war *would* come, but put its outbreak at the end of 1940. I tended to agree. He surprised me by asking if people in England thought that Churchill would take over as prime minister in the event of war. It was the first I had ever heard of such a suggestion.

On the course of the war he was also very interesting, again testing me as to English and particularly undergraduate views. He thought France would collapse quickly. This again came as a complete surprise to me and I was able to say truthfully that I had never heard such a suggestion.

He considered that Russia would remain neutral. I hazarded the opinion that she would ally with Germany. He said that in any event America would have to come in and that would defeat Germany: what did people in England think? I said I supposed they thought that.

Arising from his view as to the inevitability of that, he expressed the opinion that Hitler could avoid war by not grasping too much, but he felt that he would press too far. He did not say in what direction.

He conversed on a number of other things apart from war, particularly politics and religion. Did I not think there would be a wave of socialism in England? I did. He then asked in detail about English views on its consequences—for example, nationalisation. With my experience of the Oxford Union I was able to give him a picture of under-graduate—and indeed general English—reactions, which corresponded closely to his own forecasts and, as it turned out, the fact.

He asked me in detail about my own plans and expressed no surprise at all at my decision to practice at the English Bar. He said nothing about my family connection with the Law and nothing by way of asking why I would not be practising entirely at the Irish Bar. The nearest he went to any kind of suggestion was to ask if I had considered the Irish diplomatic. It had never occurred to me till then and I rather brushed it aside. It never occurred to me then that the suggestion might indeed have been an invitation.

Anyway I never followed it up. Perhaps I should have. But my heart had always been set on the Bar.

After this long meeting I never met or heard from Dev again.

I wondered at the time if I should mention my father and Uncle Michael but saw no point in doing so when he—to my surprise—most markedly did not. Looking back on the whole thing, that was the point which struck me most; that, and the intimate knowledge he had about me. Also, his obvious deep affection for my mother. What view did I form of him? I thought he was a shrewd and calculating man with all the mind of the top mathema-tician that he was. An exceptionally well-informed man. A statesman but one who was a semi-dictator. A person who knew only one position, that of Leader. A man who would not tolerate opposition and moreover would not respect it. A deep-thinking, quick-thinking interrogator. A mag-netic personality.

Uncoloured by my family's then view of him, I saw that
he had little place for lawyers and no great appreciation
for conventional law. He was not a very attractive speaker
nor indeed a very attractive personality, but he was a com-
pelling man who left me with admiration for the scope of
his mind and the command of his person. He had a mag-
netism which was attributed to no attractiveness of appearance, manner or approach but simply to overall command.

Why had he sent for me?—because that is what he did.
I think it was partly curiosity and interest, born of his
experience at Beaufield. And partly to check through me
on his own information about English reactions; as it happened he was very well informed. Far better informed
than Hitler or Mussolini. Far ahead of much of English
thinking at the time.

His height and build and features—his bad eyesight
too—helped to make him a remarkable man that he
clearly was. A genius. A commander.

I had thought of mentioning my father, in a way which
might prompt Dev to give him some judicial appointment,
but Daddy (a man of quick temper and brilliant invective)
had said some harsh and bitter things about Dev, which
had surely got back to him. They were in the context of
the breach with Uncle Michael. Dev was not a forgiving
man, so (like him) I made no mention of father or uncle.

6

With the BBC and as a Pupil at the Bar

WHILE AT OXFORD I DECIDED to make my future principally in England, at the English Bar, rather than at the Irish Bar—though I intended, and in fact carried out the intention, to do some legal work in Ireland and certainly to carry on Belvin. I think that at this time my father as well as my aunts and uncles would have preferred me, as the sole young male of the family, to return to Ireland permanently, but they respected my own wishes and were pleased that I managed through the whole of my life in England to make weekends in Ireland at least twice a month and sometimes more often. This was not only pleasurable but increasingly necessary in order that I should begin to run Belvin for my father and aunts.

Decided upon England as the career country and possessed unfortunately of recurrent attacks of deep depression aptly known as 'Black Dog', my path was guided by the Ministry of Labour to the BBC, who agreed to take me upon leaving Oxford into their 'Empire Service', a wartime service which covered the English-speaking world and was in effect a skilful propaganda department broadcasting regular news bulletins, talks and features. However, I was unable to take up my employment for some months because of an attack of 'Black Dog', which I spent in hospital in Ireland. It was incidentally an Oxford friend, Eleanor Murphy (Mrs John Holmes), who introduced me to that grim and apt term.

I had already done my bar exams at Oxford with the traditional help of the well-known correspondence school of Gibson and Weldon.

I was thus enabled shortly after joining the BBC to get called to the Bar by the Inner Temple, at the earliest possible age of twenty-one. I remember that I got a 'bisque' for the purpose; a pleasant BBC practice— borrowed I imagine from golf—of allowing so many days off in a year on application, provided working circumstances permitted. I used periodically get one to lengthen a weekend at home in Ireland.

The BBC Empire Service took me on as a sub-editor in the news room, principally concerned with sub-editing the news but periodically preparing, periodically broadcasting, features and talks. I was sent for three months training to the BBC Training Centre at Aldenham, just in the country outside North London. It was held in the very pleasant premises of Aldenham School, which had been taken over for the war by the BBC. Those of us on the course were billeted on unfortunate householders in the outlying suburbs of Stanmore and Edgeware and collected and left back by a coach which had set meeting points. I was billeted with a very nice couple in Stanmore, just a few minutes walk from one of the coach stopping places.

The Empire Service was based at premises taken over from Peter Robinson's at 200 Oxford Street in London, just near Oxford Circus. As with Broadcasting House itself (BH) there were a number of deep basements from which broadcasting could be carried on entirely safe from bombs. Entry to the broadcasting areas was marshalled by an army sentry to whom, however well known one was, you had to produce a photographed identity card every time.

The editors and most of the sub-editors were experienced Fleet Street men, and women, and the regular news readers were mostly actors. The typists—I remember particularly a Miss Carpenter—were amongst the speediest shorthand-typists I have ever encountered or even heard of. The whole team was very stimulating and interesting to work with, and the method of writing required was in very marked distinction to the style one had become accustomed to at school and university. I remember on a number of occasions having had words of mine altered as being 'too academic'.

Covering all areas of the globe we naturally had to do shift work to cope with a 24-hour period. We also had to become accustomed to changing words and whole phrases to meet the usage of whatever country was on a particular programme. Thus—and I can use the word here without fear of correction—I remember that 'a goods train' became 'a freight train' for countries such as Canada.

The programmes were of course 'Allied-angled' and avowedly propaganda. We were conscious of exaggeration of Allied gains and diminishing of Allied losses but not— at any rate we thought then—to a very great extent.

If I were of any special use, I suppose it was to angle things for Irish listeners throughout the world. I was conscious of being 'used' but certainly not 'abused'.

I lodged off Baker Street, and it was not any spirit of bravery which made me sleep in my bed-sitting room rather than make use of the bunks in the Underground stations. It was a distaste of the whole atmosphere down there. Nearly everybody in my street took refuge in the Underground at night.

I experienced bombing around my lodgings, but none particularly near. Perhaps the oddest experience I had was on an occasion returning from work when I helped to put out fires caused by fire-bombs in an empty unoccupied house off Oxford Street (most of the houses around there were unoccupied at that time and would indeed have been purchasable at what would now look ridiculously cheap figures). The point of my story is that unknown to us— most certainly unknown to us—there was a landmine in the house, which demolished it completely next day.

While with the BBC I began in the latter part of 1944 to do some part-time pupillage in the Temple when I had daylight hours off duty; and, correspondingly, when I left the BBC for whole-time pupillage I continued to do work for them. I was fortunate to find as pupil-master Edward Holroyd Pearce of Fountain Court in the Temple (known affectionately as E.H.P.). He eventually became a law lord. A delightful and wonderful man, to whom I owe much, it was my good fortune to be kept on as a tenant, and after we moved to nearby Queen Elizabeth Buildings I became head of chambers myself. I had E.H.P.'s son Bruce as a pupil of mine.

When I was with the BBC there were many incidents and crises, but what impressed me most—and I am sure it is still the case in BBC Radio and Television—is that programmes, particularly the News, gave such an appearance of punctual, unhurried efficiency when in fact from the state of affairs in the news room it seems miraculous that the bulletin should get out on time and so smoothly at all.

My particular bosses on the Empire News were Frank Singleton, who had been editor of the *Bolton Evening News*, and a Mr Rumson and a Mr Dick, who had held important positions in Fleet Street.

We got our news principally from the Reuter and Exchange Telegraph tape-service, but we had reporters too and sometimes ourselves acted as reporters and interviewers.

We had a canteen, which was very useful. It was the scene of one of the amusing incidents I remember. A member of the Afrikaans staff, the worse for drink, poured his soup over the cook. When summoned disciplinarily for this, he ran the defence—an unavailing one, I may say— that the soup was cold and that that was the cause, and a good cause, for what he did (moreover it meant that the cook was not scalded). I do not recall the precise penalty meted out to him. It certainly was not dismissal (he was too irreplaceable for that). I think he had to pay something by way of compensation to the cook and had some leave stopped.

On occasions, I felt very important with the BBC—when I was deputed to act as censor (everything that went out had to be censored) and when I was required to act for a period as night editor. Given a bit of luck, I thought, I might become one of the bosses!

Master and Pupil

Part of a pupil's duty is to 'cover' for his master, that is to say, watch in a court where the master is due to come on shortly while he finishes in another court. The pupil has to 'hold the fort' even if it involves the unpopular course of asking the judge to 'give my learned friend a few minutes'. If the judge declines, or the delay becomes excessive, you are all right if it is for the other side to open the case, but if it is for your side to do so, you are in dead trouble. The only thing then is to get your liaising clerk to summon your master straight away, whatever his position in the other court. Telling a judge that your master is 'in difficulties' does not mention that unfortunately you feel in even greater difficulties. Still (funnily enough) good luck, and good clerking, as by our Clement Mulhern, somehow usually get round the crisis.

In 'covering' I once managed to lose my master, Edward Holroyd Pearce, good clients. I was summoned from beside him in court and told by our clerk to get to a certain divorce court and on his behalf agree £4,000 damages and costs, against a co-respondent. The case had just started there and I literally sprinted along the intervening corridors, muttering '£4,000 damages and costs'. I arrived out of breath and heard the judge say, 'Ah, I see that somebody has come on behalf of Mr Holroyd Pearce.'

I said, rather unnecessarily, 'I have, my Lord.'

'Yes, Mr. . . Mr Umph,' he said kindly.

'I've come', I said quickly, afraid of forgetting my lines, 'to agree to £4,000 damages and costs against the co-respondent.' There it was—mission accomplished.

The judge, however, was not finished. 'Now, that's strange Mr. . . Mr Umph', he replied, 'because I was just telling your opponent that I did not think adultery had been proved against the co-respondent.'

I was shaken, but only momentarily. I was determined to do my duty to the letter. 'I can't help that', I said. 'Does your lordship seriously think we'd be agreeing £4,000 and costs if the co-respondent hadn't committed adultery with the wife?', and I added 'frequently' for good measure.

The judge paused for a moment. Then with the ghost of a smile he said, 'You've convinced me, Mr Umph. Decree, damages and costs.'

The solicitors never came back to my master.

Two Bundles

My master in the law, E.H.P., taught me early on good things which I have never forgotten and which I have used myself ever since. Many sets of documents and many briefs contain an excessive amount of papers (I remember one set of papers which, inexplicably, contained twelve copies of the writ). My task with a big set of papers was to divide the papers into neat bundles, one called the Balls Bundle (tied up and meant to be referred to never again) and the other the Real Bundle.

Finding One's Feet

There were various ways in which the pupil and young barrister sought to find his feet. I did so in company with two of my chambers friends and contemporaries, both future lord justices, Robin Dunn and Roger Ormond.

One method was Applications. In the Queen's Bench division these were then made at ten minutes to one, to the Senior QB judge, who was at the time Mr Justice Hilbery. The applications were usually to adjourn a case which was about to come into the list—for good or spurious reasons. Mr Justice Hilbery was ill-disposed to standing cases out of the list, however good the reason, and even if the application was not opposed (or actively consented to) by the other side.

As a junior E.H.P. had up to sixty sets of papers on his desks for attention. Part of my duty as his devil being to check papers, many caused amusement but none the laughter that greeted a typist's error: 'The petitioner has frequently committed adultery with the Queen's Proctor.'

One application which I made on behalf of my master was that a case due for the next day should be postponed because our client, the plaintiff, was unwell. I handed in one of these rather unsatisfactory pro forma medical certificates which said that the lady was unfit for work because of hypertension. Hilbery looked at it with disdain and cast it from him saying, 'She'll be well in the morning.' She was.

On another occasion, again for Edward Holroyd Pearce, I applied to stand a case out from the next day, this time because we had been caught by surprise and our client was unavailable because she was in the Dublin mountains. 'I know them well', said Mr Justice Hilbery. 'Send her a telegraph now and she can be on the night packet. She will be at Euston Station three hours before the court sits tomorrow.'

In an application on my own behalf I applied on the usually hopeless ground that I had another case specially fixed for tomorrow. It was certainly an unusual circumstance to have two of one's only cases clashing. Mr Justice Hilbery was sympathetic to a young man (he had almost got my name right by that time), but he said, No—the case must be in the list 'without fail' tomorrow. My splendid clerk Clement saw behind the scenes that his lordship's edict was carried out—but that the case was listed behind the longest action then pending. Thus it remained for a day or two before I was able to do it.

There were also 1.30 summonses before Queen's Bench masters, dealing with interlocutory (interim) matters about cases and finally disposing of any prospect of lunch. Edward Holroyd Pearce often had about five of them and I would do perhaps two of them for him. They were held in what was known as the Bear Garden because it resembled a bear garden with myriads of people milling around trying to get into the master's room. It was a very unsatisfactory procedure, with speed of the essence and three or five minutes the norm ('Running down action, Master'—pushing the papers at him—'Want trial at Winchester. Accident there. Plaintiff in hospital there. Friend wants London.' Friend intervenes, 'All experts in London.' Master adjudicates briskly, 'Trial London.' Or, 'Want summary judgment, Master. Friend's affidavit no real defence.' Friend hands it in. Master skims through it, 'Just enough. Leave to defend'.) The practice has happily been altered now and there are special appointments fixed during the day.

Then there were magistrates' courts and county courts throughout London, giving one a variety of cases—and of tribunals.

In the magistrates' courts there were affiliation and matrimonial cases, assaults, drunks, breaches of the peace, assorted stealing (pickpockets, shoplifting, stealing from employers etc.), travelling on public transport without paying the proper fare, miscellaneous motoring offences, indecencies, etc. Most were pleas of Guilty with elaborate pleas in mitigation. The occasional fight brought the even more occasional win, which was very satisfactory. Motorists were the most belligerent but usually had no defence, their anger really being at being caught.

In the county court in my day my staple diet was appearing for debtors (usually on judgment enforcement summonses brought by hire-purchase companies) and in Rent Act possession actions, of which there were many after the war, when accommodation was woefully scarce.

It was astonishing how much some people had on hire-purchase and how much arrears some accumulated, but a promise to keep up current payments and to pay so much a week off the arrears usually managed to keep the goods.

In the cases where the tenant had Rent Act possession it was possible for the landlord to claim possession on certain specified grounds, of which the most usual were 'greater hardship' (to the landlord if refused possession than for the tenant if ordered to leave) and 'alternative accommodation' (that there was suitable alternative accommodation for the tenants, offered by the landlord or otherwise available.)

In hardship cases mothers-in-law, usually in bad health, were regularly brought into play by both sides; also grandfathers (frequently crippled), aunts, unmarried sisters, widowed sisters (who contributed financially and by nursing), old friends of the family who had always lived with them, dogs, cats and of course the children's pet budgerigar. Wonder was that one suburban house—or flat—could contain so many or on the other side could be required for so many. Then naturally it would be near the landlord's work and would enable his wife to get part-time work there too. The tenant argued that it was near his work—that there was nowhere to be got anywhere else and no less than three of his family worked within three-quarters of a mile. So the pendulum of hardship swung to and fro.

When the claim for possession was on the ground of suitable alternative accommodation, the landlord painted a picture of it that would make an estate agent envious. He could not understand why the tenant did not leap at it. (In such a case I often wondered why the landlord did not take it himself.) The tenant, however, saw it all with different eyes. It was too dangerous for the children, it was in bad repair, the best supply of water was from the leaking roof, the electricity needed rewiring, there was wet and dry rot, and rising damp, the floorboards were unsafe and there were evil smells from a nearby factory.

Judge Donald Hurst at Bromley and points south used to put landlord and tenant at opposite sides in front of him and fire questions at them in turn: 'Nature of your work?' 'Where?' 'How much?' 'How many children?' 'Ages?' 'Any ailing?' Counsel were allowed to intervene.

I got a good deal of my county court work at Brentford before Judge Tudor Rees from Mr Knightley of Ferris and Reed. A middle-aged lady reporter attended his court assiduously and got a small regular income from the double-paged *Evening News*, which specialised in snippets on its front page, many of which were Judge Tudor Rees' *obiter dicta*. Occasionally she got a proper story, even a scoop, as when in a claim for possession of a stable he gave a horse six months to find alternative accommodation.

It was this learned judge's custom to run through his list first thing to find what was in it and enable him to take the short cases first. He used to ask us in turn and knew our reliability by experience. Calling over the last of the longest cases in the list, he used to say. 'It could be three months before I try your case. But if you agree you can be tried by the registrar straight away.' I always resisted the temptation.

Now, there was a leading case called *Neale and Del Soto* which decided that if a tenant shared a kitchen he had no Rent Act protection. It came as a surprise to us practitioners but led to a lot of disputes and litigation. On one occasion when the judge was running through the list, a solicitor when called upon for his estimate said, 'Very short, Your Honour. I propose to *Neale and Del Soto* the Defendant.' This had a bloodthirsty and chilling sound about it at the time and ever since I have regarded the case as a blood-curdling one.

Judge Tudor Rees had an usher who used to let out robes, wing-collars and bands to visiting solicitors. He could similarly oblige barristers who had forgotten some item of court dress. But solicitors were his speciality, and I think his charges were moderate, something like five shillings (25p.) a day. On one occasion a plaintiff's name was called and a man stepped into the witness-box dressed in solicitor's robes. 'Are you a solicitor?' enquired the judge. 'No.' 'Then why are you dressed like a solicitor?' 'Well', explained the litigant, 'I wandered into the robing room upstairs and that chap there,'—pointing to the then disappearing usher—'offered to fit me out with proper robes. When he said that, I thought everyone had to have robes.' He was told to go away and undress. The usher was sent for but never materialised. I met him on subsequent occasions at Brentford County Court but his robing business had ceased.

At Whitechapel County Court I remember finding on the door of the judge's court a notice saying, 'No spitting'. It was a surprising notice to find and I confess to feeling that it would never have occurred to anybody to spit had there not been a notice about it.

The judge at Westminister was Basil Blagden, a delightful man. It was generally believed that he would have got preferment had he not made jokes in court. The one usually cited was his definition to a jury of circumstantial evidence: 'If you see a man coming out of a pub wiping his mouth, that is circumstantial evidence that he has been having a drink, but it is not conclusive evidence: he may have been kissing a barmaid.'

Having a wry sense of humour myself, I have always liked the story about Basil Blagden at Sloane Square underground station. By the escalator there was—still is—a notice saying 'Dogs Must Be Carried'. Basil sought out a porter and said, 'Forgive me, I'm in difficulty.' 'Oh, yes, sir.' 'That notice says, "Dogs Must Be Carried"—but I have no dog.'

Similarly, confronted by a sign which said, 'No Waiting or Loading', he asked a police officer whether the prohibition was conjunctive or separative.

County courts, particularly my regular Brentford, remind me of the opulent leader who once told me that he had one basic rule about investments. When acting for a company he always bought shares in it. I remember thinking first how lucky he was to have the money to do so—even when they paid his fees. I certainly couldn't follow his example. And anyway what portfolio would ever contemplate Brentford Bootlaces Ltd, or Bangers of Brentford Inc., or even Cucumbers of Kew. Indeed many of my company clients were either already in liquidation or were so deeply debentured that even the oldest employee could not remember when they last paid a dividend.

My First Case

Uncle Michael wrote charmingly of his first case: 'It was a bad case and I did it badly.' I could say of mine that it was a good case and I did it badly.

In those pre-Legal Aid days there was a pleasantly named Catholic society called the Society of our Lady of Good Counsel, which provided free legal aid, and for court appearances paid the barrister out of its own resources one guinea. I came to know the society early in my days of pupillage and they sent me my first case. I did it on a day off from the BBC.

It was an affiliation summons at Bow Street by an Italian girl against an Italian man in his early twenties. She was detailed and convincing to me and to the court, but we lacked sufficient corroboration—that is to say, independent supporting evidence. (I should probably have stressed the need more strongly before the hearing.) We lost—I'm still quite sure unjustly. They submitted no case to answer and the plea succeeded so that the father—yes, father—was able to leave court smirking without having had to give evidence. I was very hurt by the defeat.

There is a story told of an affiliation case with an equal paucity of corroboration where the chairman of the Bench later told the putative father's counsel how they had managed to find the case proved. 'The baby was the image', he said, 'of your client sitting below there in court.' 'Good God', replied the barrister, 'my client wasn't even in court. That was my instructing solicitor.'

Despite initial failure the society continued to brief me. In one case I had to make seven successive Saturday appearances before an irascible compatriot, Mr McKenna, at Bow Street—all for the same guinea. It all arose because in my youthful ingenuity I had entered 'a plea in bar' for my client, namely that he had previously been convicted of what was really the same offence. Mr McKenna put numerous difficulties in my path and kept adjourning me from Saturday to Saturday for further argument. Eventually after about five Saturdays I told him in exasperation that I would withdraw my plea and alter it to one of Guilty. With what I felt was a touch of sadism, he refused to accept that course and said—I believe inaccurately— that it was not possible. So the farce proceeded and on the seventh Saturday he rejected the submission. We then pleaded Guilty at last and were fined, I think, five pounds. A thoroughly baffled client was much pleased. My feeling was one of relief and grateful release.

My second case, however, had been much briefer. It was a 'dock brief' at the Old Bailey. Again almost a relic of pre-Legal Aid days, it enabled anyone with £1.3s.6d. to choose any barrister in court to represent him for that sum. Many tried to avoid being chosen, for example by attempted disappearance from court. Not me. My sole purpose of being in court was to try to be chosen for a dock brief. And unlike others I did not mind how long the case lasted. In fact it turned out to be inevitably a plea of Guilty. The charge was stealing and the prisoner had been caught red-handed. My task therefore was reduced to a plea of mitigation. I say 'reduced to' but *a plea in mitigation is in fact one of the most difficult aspects of advocacy*. On this occasion I think I accidentally achieved a small reduction in sentence. It was by unintentionally making an unsmiling Judge Beazley actually laugh.

I had prepared an eloquent plea. It was pretty factual stuff to start with but then at the climax came this: 'And now he has the ultimate and appalling disgrace of being represented by me and of appearing before you today.'

An amused judge turned to me and in time-honoured fashion said, 'Thank you, Mr Comyn, you've said everything that can be said.' That is a conventional but often ominous phrase, suggestive of an unfavourable aftermath. Not so, I think here.

It is nice to have one's name actually mentioned in court in the early days. Handing it in on a piece of paper enables this, even if it does not ensure the proper pronunciation.

The early days saw little advisory or drafting work of one's own but plenty via and for my master. I got high payment, two guineas, for drafting a lease. It worried me greatly and took me a lot of time but it must have been all right because I heard of no repercussions. I consulted every precedent I could find, including one which (from the last century) restricted the tenant to four horses and two carriages. This was a third-floor self-contained flat in Eaton Place.

Beginners in our chambers like me often got briefs which came endorsed to our clerks. Thus, 'For one of Arthur Smith's (or Clement Mulhern's) young men.' It was up to you to get the next one in your own name.

A Very Rude Judge

Once upon a time there was a Rude Judge. A Very Rude Judge. It really seemed as if he could not help being rude, to everybody, always, in court and in private.

Edward Holroyd Pearce feared few but feared him—for what might happen to his clients.

On one occasion in court, a crowded court, E.H.P. when addressing this judge happened to say, 'But of course your Lordship knows more about engineering than I do.' Whereupon the judge actually said, 'I know more about *Everything*, Mr Holroyd Pearce, than you do.'

Then one Friday evening E.H.P. was going up Middle Temple Lane, carrying a suitcase in each hand, bound for a taxi to take him to Victoria Station for a train to take him to his country house at Crowborough in Sussex; I was accompanying him to get a taxi for him. During the week he lived in a flat above chambers at Fountain Court or, periodically, at the Athenaeum Club, of which incidentally he kindly made me a member, where we often worked together late into the night.

Half way up Middle Temple Lane we met the judge, walking down from the Strand.

'Good evening, Judge.'

'Good evening, Pearce.'

'I'm sorry I can't raise my hat to you, Judge. I have a suitcase in both hands.'

The judge eyed him coldly.

'You could put one of them down', he said.

I'm glad to say E.H.P. didn't.

It was said of Mr Justice Hilbery that he once met that extraordinary, very able, man, D. N. Pritt QC in Gray's Inn and admired his dog.

'A lovely dog you have there, Pritt.'

'Yes, Judge, but like all aristocratic looking creatures, very difficult.'

'Pritt', Hilbery J used to say, 'is, I regret to say, a very common man.'

No Safe

Whilst a pupil of E.H.P., I did with him certain secret Government work. We were warned to keep the papers in

our safe—but we had no Safe! So we used to hide the
papers in places such as behind the books in one of the
bookshelves.

Being led by E.H.P.

E.H.P. was twelve years in silk before becoming a judge
and I had the pleasure of devilling for him and frequently
being led by him during that period.

It took, I believe, two years to clear up his junior work
to the point of trial. Then there was the new work coming
on. No longer sixty sets of papers awaiting attention, but
twenty; mostly weighty and complicated matters.

There was one splendid incident of which I only heard
the details much later. Arthur Smith, our senior clerk at the
time, came into E.H.P.'s room and beckoned me out. He
had a brief in his hands, and passed it over to me, saying,
'This is a return of Norman Birkett's. It's for you and Mr
Pearce—six hundred for him and a hundred and fifty for
you. An opinion—but it must be ready first thing tomorrow, without fail. Have a read of it and then have a word
with Mr Pearce as soon as you can.'

I read it. It seemed a pretty straightforward detinue
(detention of goods) claim by our husband and wife clients,
who seemed to have the right end of it.

I went into E.H.P. between consultations and told him
exactly what Arthur had said, including the remuneration
and 'wanted tomorrow morning'.

E.H.P. said, 'Keep the next Con. back a quarter of an
hour and I'll look through it. Don't tell me your view until
I've read it.'

Within the quarter of an hour E.H.P. put down the
papers and said, 'Well?'

'Good claim', I said, 'one or two things, to be done.'

'I agree entirely. What's the money side of it?'

'£1,000 for detention and £10,000 value.'

'A bit more for the detention,' said E.H.P. 'It included stuff they could have been using. Up it to £1,700.'

We arranged that I would do a draft opinion and over-night E.H.P. would do the final opinion in his own hand and we would both sign it.

The joint opinion was ready and cheques handed over next morning. Within a month we heard that our clients' claim had been satisfactorily settled, and thank you again.

It was Clement who told me ages afterwards that Mr Norman Birkett certainly had not returned the papers. Arthur had outwitted Bowker, Birkett's clerk. Having heard from the solicitors about the case, he said that as a special favour he would get Bowker to get Birkett's opin-ion for £1,000 though Bowker would hold out for £1,250. 'Start at £500 but stick at £1,000,' he said. He then went to see Bowker and told him to stick at £1,250, which he happened to known the clients would gladly pay. Bowker thanked him profusely. Next day the solicitor told Arthur he could get nowhere with Birkett's clerk. 'Don't worry about him any more,' said Arthur. 'I've got two top men here, Mr Pearce and Mr Comyn—you known them—who'll do it for you for £750—overnight.'

In another matter there was an ancient solicitor whom we called Hodge. He early took the commendable view that in every case, however trivial, he should brief me, led by E.H.P. He was a good solicitor, practising on his own and with a lot of court work. He prepared his cases excellently and we had a good record for him.

One day in E.H.P.'s room I opened a big set of papers from Hodge named as usual for both of us. I got a pro-found shock and went over to E.H.P. at his desk.

'Why have you got a face as long as Harley Street?' he asked.

'A case from Hodge. He's the plaintiff himself.'

'Whatever for?'

'Possession of pigsties, at his place in Essex, and he's done all the pleadings himself.'

'What grounds?'

'Well, basically that they smell.'

'Pigs do smell. Old Hodge must have known that when he let the pigsties.'

'They create a lot of dirt, too.'

'Naturally. What did he think they were—pet poodles? How many are there anyway?'

'Two hundred and fifty.'

'What! And I suppose they grunt all night near his house.'

'Exactly. They're only seven hundred and fifty yards from the house.'

We then discussed whether the requisite notices and so forth were in order. There were, alas, a number of irregularities and also some unfortunate correspondence.

'I don't like the sound of it,' said E.H.P. 'Get him along and we'll talk some sense into him.'

We simply couldn't. He absolutely insisted on going on with the case. 'This is a cast-iron winner,' he said. 'Take it from me.'

We drew Mr Justice Hilbery. Ill-luck tends to attract ill-luck.

We decided to call Hodge quickly and let him present his own case. That he was very deaf did not help. That the learned judge did not approve of solicitors of the Supreme Court 'dabbling in pigs' did not help either. As time went on, long before we got to the highly arguable notices and pleadings, it became plain that his Lordship had no room for our client. Among his observations (which it is doubtful if Hodge heard) were, 'This decent tenant is presumably paying you a hefty rent. If you let property for pigs outside your bedroom window you must expect to lose some sleep', and, worst of all, 'Are you proposing to turn this horde of pigs and their young on to the highway?'

Then, as to the notices and pleadings, poor Hodge got judicial hell. Hilbery suggested he was cheese-paring in not going to me to settle them. Hodge was in fact one of the least cheese-paring people I knew.

Eventually this awful curse drew to its close. The judge began his judgment. 'This is an absurd claim by an absurd solicitor, who seems to me to be verging on senility.'

Hodge was sitting behind me and at that point tapped me on the shoulder and, in a voice which rang round the court, said, 'Is he still with us?'

E.H.P. turned quickly and said, 'James, get that man out of court. I don't care what you do with him but get him out of here.'

Later in the corridor Hodge said, 'We'll appeal.'

E.H.P. said quickly, 'Mr Comyn and I won't.'

We heard no more about the pig case. Hodge got over his period of aberration, resumed his meticulous practice and continued to brief me and E.H.P. together.

7

Old Friends

Moving from Fountain Court

ROBERT JOHNSON, EDWARD CAZALET, Michael Connell and John Hamilton became welcome additions to chambers. The two former are High Court judges now, Michael Connell is head of chambers, and John Hamilton is a Circuit Court judge. I had the pleasure of leading all of them many times.

Shortly after Edward Holroyd Pearce became a High Court judge, and when Harry Phillimore (later Lord Justice Phillimore) was head of chambers, our landlords, the Middle Temple, asked us to vacate Fountain Court and said they would give us instead a whole floor (a double set of chambers) in newly-constructed Queen Elizabeth Building, some 350 yards away—by the Embankment and the River. There, years later, as head of chambers, I had quite the finest room in the Temple, looking over the busy Embankment on to the River Thames, with a large Oxo advertisement on the far side winking at me at night.

We were all very upset and very apprehensive at being asked to leave Fountain Court. It was our home, and we feared losing 'Cat Goodwill'. We knew about 'Cat Goodwill' from our landlord and tenants. A cat will always, it is found, go back to his or her own home rather than anywhere else.

Fountain Court was a deplorable pre-Dickensian place inside. There was one really good room; the one looking out on the Fountain. It was the head of chambers' room. Behind it was a small, dingy room, which Robin Dunn and I when sharing it called the 'Escape Chamber'. We actually managed to hold conferences of our own in it, one leaving when the other had a conference.

To get to the clerk's room one had to go along a dark, cold, often wet, stone passage, a tunnel (two rooms opening off it), up two flights of often weeping stone stairs.

Around the clerk's rooms were other rooms—F.S. Laskey's (Frank Laskey's) room, which Christopher Besley (later a metropolitan magistrate) used, and Malcolm Wright's room. We lost delightful Malcolm Wright, our great Circuit lynch-pin, first to the County Court Bench, where he soon went to Westminister, obviously *en route* to the High Court up the road; and then we lost him altogether; he died young. To everyone's pleasure his son, Peter is now a member of chambers. On the floor upstairs there were two large rooms. Blanco White QC, of shaky hand and an enormous yellow fountain pen, occupied one, and Roger Ormrod (later Mr Justice, later again Lord Justice, Ormrod) shared it with him.

In the other were Jim Hale, David Moylan, Roger Gray and after Jim Hale me, and all other members of chambers and pupils, except Donald McIntyre, who later became a county court judge, and Dougall Lord Meston.

Donald McIntyre inhabited a 'shoot off' room on the ground floor, a room which looked out on Essex Street. Beside it was the most extraordinary room in chambers— in the whole of the Temple, I would imagine. It was about twenty feet long by ten feet wide. There was a very old, noisy, half broken, gas fire on the right-hand side wall, right-hand as one walked in. The desk was at the end of the room.

I got this room—all to myself alone—on my first 'promotion' in chambers. I was immensely proud of it. I put up three large pictures; one of Daddy in full robes; one of the aunts; one of Belvin. I bought an expensive carpet ('very odd dimensions, if I may say so, sir', said the carpet-man I bought it from). I bought a grand desk (at Christie's, with E.H.P.'s help). Also an elegant desk chair, again with E.H.P.'s help and advice.

Having a conference in that room necessitated having the solicitor in one chair, a couple of feet ahead of the lay client in another chair, and if there was anybody else (and there was usually at least a pupil) he had another chair (again bought separately), another couple of feet back below the lay client. It was not possible to have two chairs side by side. Whoever had the second chair (the lay client's chair) got his or her right side roasted in Winter time by the gas fire.

There was an ancient, dirty, unmoveable window behind me, which had crinkled glass to stop people in Essex Street looking in. For the eighteen months or so that I was in it I loved that room. It marked my second great step at the English Bar. It was *my* room. I missed my old room-mate Robin Dunn very much (he then had the 'Escape Chamber' to himself), but I no longer had to move out when he had a Con.

It was in that room that I received my pre-dawn clients in the Tank Con (see Chapter 8).

Across the stone passage was a large room, occupied by Lord Meston. Amongst other things he wrote guides to new statutes.

Once, to his surprise, in an idle moment I called in on him and offered to write, for a small fee, notes to (a) the part which said that this Act did not apply to Scotland or Northern Ireland and (b) the short title section. In his guides, I pointed out, he had not hitherto had any notes at all on these important provisions. I said that in my view they called for careful, lengthy, annotation. For example under (a) I would list the counties of Scotland and the Six Counties of Northern Ireland, and elaborate on them; and under (b) I would list and contrast the short titles of similar statutes in Ireland, Australia, New Zealand, Germany and France—but not, I stressed—the United States of America. I spoke solemnly and with a straight face. 'Think about it, Dougall', I said. He was a very nice man. I then popped back into my room. Alas, nothing came of my suggestion.

If my little room was crowded with pupils or visiting members of chambers on a gossip and Clement wanted to get some papers to me, he used to stay at the entrance to the room and throw them at me.

Actually at the time the senior clerk was still old Arthur Smith, the doyen clerk of the Temple, about whom every known barristers' clerks story was told. He was about six foot tall, with a handsome face and very ruddy cheeks. He was always dressed in smart, conventional, barrister's dress, a black jacket and waistcoat, with quiet pin-stripe trousers. He did not, however, wear a winged collar. He always wore a lovely white shirt and a 'quiet' tie. He was handsome and increasing grey hair increased his handsomeness.

He was a Freemason; high up in the Masons. He recruited Clement and many members of chambers, but not me. He and Clement were very tolerant of me not being a Mason, and used to invite me to Ladies' Nights, where I was not at all surprised to find several solicitors' managing clerks. I found Ladies' Nights—which were an entirely new experience for me—very enjoyable but exceedingly long; 5.30 p.m. to 12.30 a.m. I was invariably asked to speak at the dinner; to respond for The Guests. I have never been a good after dinner speaker and it always caused me great anxiety. Which is, I suppose, strange when I never, ever, felt any sort of nerves of any kind about speaking in any court in the land—once I was on my feet.

Arthur Smith was an accomplished after-dinner speaker and used to tell us 'the art' of it—a total of between ten and fifteen minutes; a few pleasantries to start with, then a few facts and a few tactful general comments, finally some good stories. 'When you have them rocking in the aisles— sit down.'

Queen Elizabeth Building was rather grand after Fountain Court. It had eight large rooms and a clerk's double room and a typist's room. All brand new. We did not know ourselves and found that we lost very little good will but gained a lot.

A *Voyage round John Mortimer*

The famous author and playwright John Mortimer has been a friend of mine since Oxford days. That he was brilliant with words and ideas, spoken and written, was obvious then.

When I came to the Bar, I came to know his father, who was totally blind and who was assisted in court, in the probate and divorce work which he did, by his gallant wife. He was a particular authority on probate and wrote a textbook on it which though old is still very useful and often referred to. John wrote an excellent and successful play about his father called *A Voyage Round My Father*.

The general tendency now is to regard John Mortimer as a brilliant author and playwright and from the legal point of view the creator of that wonderful character Rumpole of the Bailey. It is widely overlooked that he is in fact a QC, and though now regrettably no longer practising was brilliant in that role too.

I was often against him when we were both junior barristers and well knew his ability then. As a QC he entered the criminal courts with success in defence of alleged obscene and indecent books and publications, it being a principle dear to his heart that there should be complete freedom of publication.

When I was a judge he appeared before me in criminal cases and was most impressive, which makes me regret that he has given up the Bar completely. Even an occasional appearance in selected cases would be something to look forward to and relish.

One case he appeared in before me at the Old Bailey was an extraordinary one of alleged double murder where in a fracas a man wielding a kitchen knife with one blow killed two people. John nearly succeeded in getting a verdict of manslaughter. In the customary letter which a judge wrote to the home secretary after a murder verdict, I made a point of saying that I thought it would not be quite fair to regard the prisoner as a *double* murderer, for although wielding a lethal weapon it was in a sense accidental that it cost *two* lives.

An attractive feature of John Mortimer is his outspokeness. I was at the flattering receiving end of one instance of this when at a Law Society banquet, in the presence of my boss, the Lord Chief Justice, Lord Lane, he said that I was the only judge he had encountered who summed-up fairly. With that final touch, of which he is a master, he added, 'And that of course is the best way to make sure of a conviction.' His picture of Rumpole and supporting characters is delightful, and to those of us who know the Old Bailey there is readily detectable in all the characters a composite of Old Bailey regular practitioners and an echo of Old Bailey incidents, nicely disguised, which gives an added attraction to the series.

On many counts and particularly as writer *and* practitioner John Mortimer deserves a very special place in the law.

Bill Elverston-Trickett, Client and Friend

Bill was a solicitor, and principal of the firm of Elvy Robb and Company of King James Street in London. The 'Trickett' part of his name (which he said he thought a trifle unfortunate for a solicitor) he adopted in compliance with the will of a relative who left him all her considerable property on condition that he took or added this name. He had a brother at the Chancery Bar, who was at one time treasurer of the Middle Temple.

Bill Elverston, as I used to call him (William Marsden Eleverston Trickett), was one of my first solicitor clients

and became one of my closest friends. He had a most
wonderful sense of humour, and a feature of it was that he
gave rein to it in moments of crisis—and if it did not
always completely resolve the crisis it never failed to help
things greatly. I think this will emerge in one or two of the
matters I mention.

Bill was educated—like John Wilmers, mentioned
below—at Leighton Park School and Cambridge. Leighton
Park is a famous Quaker public school just outside Reading,
on the south western side. When I was at the Oratory we
used to play them at most games and found the boys
exceptionally nice. I had not met many Quakers myself,
but my father, who had, used to say that they were among
the finest people he had ever met and that the City of
Dublin owed much to them. Even there, he used to point
out, many of them were strangely (or is there an explanation for it?) connected with chocolate manufacturing.
In Dublin there were the Jacobs, better known in fact as
biscuit manufacturers, inventors of cream crackers, in Britain, of course, the Frys, the Cadburys and the Rowntrees.

Bill did not actively practise his religion, if that be the
right way of describing the Society of Friends, but he had
all the virtues which one associates with them—integrity,
high principles and a desire to help people and to make
this a kinder, pleasanter and juster world. He was a
bachelor, a gay bachelor, until he was over sixty, when he
married a most delightful widow of about the same age,
Lady Windlesham. She was a Catholic and he used regularly
to accompany her to Mass—often to the Brompton Oratory.
They lived in a flat in Eaton Square which was hers before
marriage. For many, many years he had lived in the
residential part of the Grosvenor House Hotel in Park
Lane, and kept the cars which he dearly loved, usually
Rolls Royces, in the hotel garage underneath.

He was an outstanding solicitor, who was principally
concerned with high-powered advisory and trustee work
for high-powered people. For example, he numbered among

his clients members of the Lloyd George and Churchill families. As a matter of fact I think that he and Megan Lloyd George (of whom Lord Morris of Borthy-y-Gest was at one time also a suitor) nearly got married. They all remained very close friends. Megan never married; nor did Lord Morris.

On behalf of the Lloyd George family I had a most unusual case from him—to apply to the Probate Court on behalf of the executors of David Lloyd George, the late prime minister, to delete from probate of his will a part consisting of some five or six sentences, non-dispositive in character, on the ground that they were scandalous and offensive. The power to do this exists in the Probate Court but is, as one might expect, rarely invoked. To tell you what we sought to delete, and why, would of course defeat the whole purpose of the exercise!

But apply I did, by way of motion, to Mr Justice Collingwood. Though not opposed by anybody, it had to be made in open court and accordingly be listed in the daily cause list. Its appearance there, as *In the Estate of David Lloyd George, Deceased*, attracted the press of the world. They certainly got a sensational item—but very little detail!

I was quickly able to satisfy the learned judge of his powers and then equally quickly that this was a classic case for exercise of them. There was some newspaper, and general, speculation, as to who was the person, or who were the persons, referred to by David Lloyd George in offensive terms in his will. This much I am entitled to say, and did in fact say in open court, that Lloyd George's first wife was *not* involved.

Bill acted, on occasions but not in general, for Winston Churchill. He acted regularly, and non-litigiously, for Clementine and for their daughter Mary and the husband she married, Lord Soames as he became. He had a very great affection for 'Clemmie' and for Mary and for Lord

Soames. He was of course the soul of discretion, but he had some good Winston stories, which included confirmation of the fact that he bought Chartwell without consulting his wife at all! Bill shared my view, which was new to him, that some of Winston's great phrases came from or were influenced by P.G. Wodehouse, of whom Bill and I were devotees.

This inevitably leads to golf, which was Bill's great passion in life. I do not know how many first-class golf clubs he belonged to, but there were several, and we played together (at regular monthly intervals) at Sunningdale, the Berkshire and Wentworth. He was a good golfer, with a handicap of no more than four or five when I first knew him, and I am pretty certain that he had been a golf blue when up at King's College, Cambridge. I was always an indifferent player; my lowest handicap was fourteen. But Bill tolerated me as an occasional partner, when we would play thirty-six holes on a Saturday.

I introduced him to Portmarnock and Lahinch in Ireland and he thoroughly enjoyed them, regarding them (rightly) as truly great courses. I remember vividly one occasion—after lunch—when he went round Portmarnock, admittedly on a calm and sunny day, in par. He dropped one stroke, at about the eighth hole, but recovered it by a birdie at the sixteenth. We also had some fun in Ireland on other, lesser, courses, including my home course, Royal Tara, a splendidly unusual course at Athlone, overlooking Lough Rea, and a fun course at Adare, in County Limerick, one of the most beautiful villages and places in Ireland.

I was able to tell him that my favourite singer, John McCormack, came from Athlone originally and was in the choir of the local church. My father remembered his debut in Dublin and remembered particularly how shy he was, 'holding his hands straight down the sides of his body'.

The Lahinch golf links (there are now two courses) are in County Clare, and the main one runs in parts beside the Atlantic. There is a fascinating hole there, the sixth, which is called 'The Dell' and is only about a hundred and seventy yards long. I can only describe it by saying that one plays into (or, rather, aims to play into) a sort of large 'flower-pot' of land. (There are in fact narrow side entrances.) A number of possible consequences ensue. One can land, or stick, on the outside of the near rim; one can get stuck on the inside of it; too strong a blow can bring one to the front of the far rim, or on the back of it; or, of course, the object of the exercise, one can land on the green and get a (fairly) certain three or a possible two. I do not think I have ever achieved a three there. I usually progress from rim to rim, climbing laboriously up them and precariously down them. Bill naturally got a three and a two on the two occasions we played this hole together. He was intrigued, too, by the infallible weather gauge at Lahinch, which was (and is) where the link's goats position themselves. If they come to the inland side of the clubhouse, rough weather from the Atlantic is on its way.

Another Lloyd George case which I did for Bill (on this occasion led by Geoffrey Lawrence QC, the successful defender of Dr Bodkin Adams) was the libel action brought by a then member of the Bar, Patrick Marrinan, against the *Daily Express* and Gwilym Lloyd George, former home secretary. Leonard Lewis QC appeared for the plaintiff, and for Beaverbrook Newspapers there was my old friend and frequent opponent, Peter Rawlinson, now Lord Rawlinson QC, who years later did the Moonies case before me.

What had happened was this. The home secretary, Gwilym Lloyd George, had authorised episodes of the always controversial 'phone-tapping. On one occasion he had authorised this in respect of telephone calls to and from a well-known criminal called Billy Hill. A few of these conversations were with Patrick Marrinan, a redoubtable barrister, who acted as counsel for Hill. Their particular conversations attracted great attention when the Bar

Council disciplinary committee obtained them for disciplinary proceedings against Patrick Marrinan, which actually led to his being disbarred. (With respect to the Bar Council, of which I later became chairman and was always an admirer, I always thought their use of these tapes as being most unfortunate.)

At any rate when the question of 'phone tapping came into the news in 1961, as it periodically did, the *Daily Express* asked the former home secretary about the Billy Hill 'phone tapping, and speaking 'off the cuff' from his home in retirement in Wales, he said he had done it 'in order to catch criminals'. This the *Daily Express* ran verbatim on its front page with suitable dramatic headlines and photographs. Patrick Marrinan not unnaturally sued for libel.

The case involved pretty well all the known defences (or attempted defences) to libel (for good measure slander as well in regard to our client); did not refer to the plaintiff; was justified in respect of those to whom it referred or was intended to refer; privilege; fair comment; etc. Both the *Express* and we were in difficulties, and we knew it. It did not help us that in the eve of trial consultation with our very nice client he at one stage for quite a long period could not remember the name of the plaintiff! Geoffrey Lawrence, and Bill, had most expressive eyes. I knew from looking at them, if I had not known before, that the case would have to be settled.

Next morning's court corridor negotiations fell to me. I found Peter Rawlinson as ever very understanding and very practical. The plaintiff, through his counsel, was not unreasonable. We eventually achieved a settlement, part of which consisted of apologies to the plaintiff in open court by both defendants. Beaverbrook Newspapers, in fact, handsomely agreed that they would pay all that was payable to the plaintiff, including costs.

In another libel action I appeared for the *Express* and Peter Rawlinson for the plaintiff. I agreed to pay "substantial damages". The judge was the inimitable, almost irrepressible, Melford Stevenson, who of course knew Peter and myself well. (He had led Peter in the sad case of Ruth Ellis, who was found guilty of murdering her pretty unsatisfactory lover and was the last woman to be hanged.) Melford was determined to tease us. He tried hard to get Peter to say what the 'substantial damages' were and indeed to say what his grand total was to date. Having failed with Peter Rawlinson he turned to, or turned on, me. I was really determined to say nothing beyond what had been agreed.

'Tell me, Mr Comyn,' Melford said, 'is there a difference between "substantial damages" and "very substantial damages".'

'I suppose there could be, my Lord.'

'And are you paying "substantial damages"?'

'Yes, my Lord.'

'Not "very substantial damages"?'

'Substantial enough, my Lord.'

And so it went on.

In court of course the learned judge had in the end to give best and to give leave for 'the record to be withdrawn'. However, in private, at lunch in the Inner Temple Melford continued for weeks to try to prise out of me how much the *Express* had had to pay. It even got to the point of his putting figures to me and asking whether he was warm! Melford had a caustic tongue and wit. He used it to the full here. But I naturally could not and would not budge. 'It was more than a farthing, Melford', I kept saying, to his immense irritation.

It was Melford who described sitting with Lord Goddard LCJ in the CCA as being 'a consenting male adult'.

Reverting to dear Bill. We had quite a few memorable cases together in court and advisory.

He came to me once in amused puzzlement with a charming client, who *knew* she owed money, some £250 or £300, shall we say to 'Harridges'. But they insisted on saying that that was not the case; the position was that they owed her £800 or £900. Bill had tried his hardest by letters to convince them of the true position, but the more he wrote the firmer and tougher their attitude became. A cheque for what they said was owing had in fact passed to and fro.

The poor lay client was worried. Bill had exercised all his skill, all his charm. What were they to do? We discussed the matter for an hour or more. Eventually, it was decided that I would then and there draft 'a stiff letter' as—pompously—coming from the pen of leading counsel.

It went something like this:

> Dear Sirs,
>
> ### Re: Mrs X
>
> Reverting to previous correspondence our Client has been so concerned about this matter that she has been with the writer to Leading Counsel, Mr James Comyn QC. He is emphatic in the advice (and indeed has drafted this letter) that you must forthwith face up to the FACTS of this matter.
>
> He and we know your high (indeed international) reputation and that you must have an accounting system second to none. But of course these things do go wrong from time to time somewhere along the line. Just a little further investigation by you will, we know, reveal that in truth and fact the position is that our client owes you some £300.
>
> A cheque from you has been passing backwards and forwards but in Leading Counsel's chambers last evening our Client drew a cheque in your favour for £300 and on getting your approval, which we readily anticipate, this will conclude the whole matter satisfactorily and you will have the cheque by return.

One unfortunate result of the impasse to date has been that our Client has felt obliged to take her valued custom elsewhere, and she will indeed be relieved to visit you again with the frequency which has been so beneficial to both sides.

Finally, should you, by any chance, continue to feel any difficulty in this matter might we respectfully suggest again that you might like to instruct your Solicitors to deal with it with us? We know them very well and have a very high regard for them.

Yours faithfully,

W.M. Elverston-Trickett
ELVY ROBB AND COMPANY

I waited—eagerly—for the reply. Trickett, damn him, refused to tell me on the telephone. A further consultation with the client was arranged. When we were assembled the Great Family Solicitor spoke.

'I regret to say, Mr Comyn, it has been no good. They are—I think the word is—intransigent. They maintain their position and absolutely refuse to go to their solicitors. They have once again sent their cheque—and here it is. What do we do now?'

The very charming client looked at me beseechingly. One thing I do know is when I am beaten. I may have been right, I may have been wrong, but it was honest advice.

'Do you every travel abroad, Mrs X?' I asked. 'To Paris, or on a short cruise or anything like that?'

'Well, I do', she said, 'when I have the money.'

'You have it now,'I said firmly.

'I propose', I said, 'here and now to draft a final letter to dispose of this matter once and for all.'

Relief showed on the client's face. Mischief on Bill's.

I wrote:

Dear Sirs,

Re: Mrs X

Thank you for your letter of the so and so.

Very well. On the express advice of Leading Counsel our Client must accept that you and your accounting system are infallible. She will accept the cheque in full and final settlement of everything outstanding between you, provided that you expressly confirm by return of post that this represents your final, definite and considered view.

If this be so—and we most earnestly ask you to pause before committing yourself—our Client will, as we say, cash your cheque, and re-commence her custom with you on the footing—if we may use the phrase—of 'starting from scratch'.

Yours faithfully, etc.

Bill took the draft. Read it. Showed it to the client. They nodded. But Bill could not restrain himself.

'Would you think of just adding a postscript, Mr Comyn?'

'Yes?'

'To the effect that the writer and leading counsel would like to open accounts with you and receive similar treatment.'

The matter was ended, as so much did with Bill, with laughter. And I understand that the client had a splendid time with the money.

Incidentally Bill was a consummate letter writer. Three incidents come to mind. One, when he wrote delightfully to another solicitor on the other side, and I think largely contributed to winning the ultimate case:

Dear Sirs,
    Dear me.

Yours faithfully, etc.

Second, after receiving a rather nasty and pompous letter from solicitor opponents, he wrote to the senior partner:

> Dear Mr A.,
> I do not think I have the pleasure of knowing you personally but in rather unusual circumstances I take the liberty of writing to you personally.
> I have received the enclosed extraordinary letter from somebody in your firm. I expect that on reading it you will, like me, not want it to be on the file of correspondence at all. So may we treat it as never having been written?
> Yours faithfully, etc.

It worked.

Third—and this appealed to our mutual senses of humour, which we readily accepted were 'fourth form'—he had been told in *August* that 'the gentleman dealing with this matter is away on holiday', and having heard nothing he wrote in the following *April*:

> I hope I am not being in any way precipitate. But by any chance has the gentleman dealing with this matter yet returned from his holiday?

Then there was the case I was going to tell you about concerning Bill himself as defendant. It was a motoring case. Before the terrifically formidable Reigate Bench (I speak naturally only of the Bench of the time). He faced four summonses—careless driving, ignoring a traffic light, driving on the wrong side of the road, exceeding the speed limit. I appreciate I do not give them their proper legal descriptions but that was their effect.

We had nice police and a nice prosecution. We had, alas, a Record.

After some lengthy discussion with the other side, we agreed that my client would plead Guilty to the last two and they would not proceed with the former two. It was all done on the footing that the last two really covered everything and that crossing the red light was anyway very debatable.

The clerk and the Bench were, I think relieved to hear that a matter which they had been notified would be fully contested and would take a long time was 'going short'.

I had given considerable thought to tactics. I was going to call Bill quite shortly before mitigating. He was a tall, impressive, attractive figure. He had a delightful voice. He was a delightful man. He was not required to take an oath. In a few sentences we managed to convey the right note of apology and what I will call, for want of any better description, 'marginality'—that he was only fractionally on the wrong side of the road and just above the speed limit. Nobody had been hurt or even inconvenienced. The Record was a little awkward. There were, if I remember rightly, three convictions for speeding and one for careless driving. We went into them in a little detail—but not too much.

I then mitigated for about five minutes. I remember I had advised, and repeated to the Bench, that my client would pay *any* sum named by the prosecution for their costs without a word of question.

The Bench retired. They consisted of one woman (youngish) and two men (oldish). The clerk retired with them, which I was glad about on this occasion because he seemed a nice chap and he seemed to like us. After ten minutes they came back. We all leapt to our feet and Bill remained on his.

The chairman said that on the Brighton Road all traffic offences were serious. This was our difficulty. And the defendant did have something on the record. This was also our difficulty. But we had faced up to it very fairly and humbly. Good. And when analysed (nice word) this did not really come to much. It could be adequately met by a fine. Five pounds on each summons—and of course costs, about which leading counsel had very fairly said there would be no difficulty whatsoever.

Deep, deep relief came over Bill and myself. And over his managing clerk, Bill Griffiths, who had said to my clerk, Clement, earlier in the week that he thought his old man was 'for the high jump this time'. But mischief entered into me, as it sometimes does.

'I wonder, Mr Chairman, if my client might have time to pay?'

Bill was almost uncontrollable. He was thrusting fivers and tenners into Griffith's hands.

The Bench were, I think, a little surprised. The case had not given an *in forma pauperis* appearance. The address, Grosvenor House Hotel; a QC and junior; etc.

Plucked fiercely by the arm, as I never before had been plucked, I turned momentarily to the lay client and then quickly to the Bench. 'I am so sorry, sir', I said, 'I have made a mistake. I'm afraid it was instinctive. I always ask for time to pay, but of course in this case there is no question.'

Everybody smiled.

Outside the court, Bill put his arm round me. 'There are times, James,' he said, 'when I could cheerfully kill you.'

We had a splendid lunch and Bill drove us back to London, safely. Next morning there was a letter in familiar writing on my desk. It just said, 'Bless you,' And it enclosed a cheque for £500. I penned a little letter to Bill and enclosed his cheque, torn up. I got our junior clerk to deliver my letter by hand.

When I came back from court that afternoon Bill rang. 'I thought you might do something like that,' he said. I was very annoyed with him, I said. He was very sorry.

He was very appreciative. Did I think my senior clerk might accept something monetary? I certainly did, but I said, 'Please don't, Bill.' My wonderful senior clerk, dear Clement, *did* receive something monetary. And he did not return it.

When on form I can occasionally cross-examine a bit. But I never even got any change on this one, either from Clement or from 'young Trickett'.

He died in 1988. He had had a very bad time with his eyes. He had a wonderful wife. Life will never be the same without him.

8

Cons

The Tank

ONE HEARS A LOT ABOUT the famous cases of famous
barristers, but quite often the most extraordinary cases
come the way of young barristers and many never get to
court and are never heard about. Such a one was the case
which confronted me soon after I was taken on in
chambers.

My clerk, who was big, entered my room, which was
tiny, and he almost filled it.

'I have fixed you a conference', he said grandly. 'A new
solicitor' (they were all new to me), 'a highly confidential
matter'.

'Splendid, Clement. When?'

'Well, that's the trouble, sir. He absolutely insisted on
5.30 a.m. tomorrow'.

'5.30 a.m.!'

'Yes. It's a bit unusual, I agree, but he insisted.'

'Unusual, Clement? Have you ever fixed a con at that
sort of time before?'

'Not that I can immediately recall', replied the imper-
turbable Clement. 'But there's nothing wrong in it.'

'What's it about?'

'I couldn't exactly make out. It all sounds very hush
hush. Something about an invention I think.'

'Invention! But I know nothing about patents!'

'You are a general practitioner, sir.'

'A very general practitioner, Clement. Still one mustn't
turn away good work, must one?'

'No, indeed', he said, who never turned away anything. 'Have we an alarm clock in chambers?'

'I'm afraid not.'

'I'll have to get one?' I said definitely. 'Can the petty cash rise to it?'

'Oh yes, I think so. After all it's a legitimate business expense. And of course we might need it again, who knows.'

'I sincerely hope not.'

'The clerks won't be here,' Clement announced firmly. 'You'll have to look after yourself.' And with that solemn announcement, he left.

So I left early plus alarm clock and went to bed. I lived reasonably near chambers and could get an all-night tube, but it still meant getting up shortly after 4 a.m., which was a good four and half hours earlier than my usual time for rising. It was November and very dark and cold but I made it to chambers shortly after 5 a.m. I placed prominently on my desk a book on patents which I had borrowed from a friend.

Sharp at 5.30 a.m. the solicitor and the client arrived. One was very tall (the solicitor), and the other very small (the client). Both remarkably in Edwardian dress and without overcoats.

'Good of you to see us at this hour,' said the solicitor.

'Not at all', I tried to give the impression that I was constantly having to have conferences at this hour; the only way to fit them all in.

'We don't want everyone to know our business', explained the solicitor.

'We don't want anyone to know our business', corrected the client.

'You see, we're afraid of being followed, Mr Comyn.'

'Followed?'

'Yes, my client and I are followed nearly everywhere we go.'

'Who by?'

'Agents.' The solicitor paused. 'British agents.'

'But good heavens why?' I was thoroughly alarmed at
what was happening. 'You're both British, aren't you?'

'Indeed', said the solicitor loyally.

'Naturally', said the client.

I misheard and thought he said 'Naturalised'. It took a
few minutes to sort that one out.

'Have you been followed this morning?' I asked.

'I think not. What do you say, Hector?'

Hector—the client—thought not too.

At last getting down to business, the solicitor said, 'We
have come to consult you about a very important matter.'
I gave the sort of bow that I felt was expected. 'You see',
went on the solicitor, 'our client here, Mr Hector Hooter
MA' (that was not his name).

'MA?'

'MA Oxon', the client intervened.

'Oh, which college?' I asked politely.

'New College.'

'So was I.'

'Before my time I expect', said the aged client.

'I was at Cambridge', the solicitor said defensively.

'Well, well, it's a small world', remarked the client.

'Yes indeed.' The solicitor cleared his throat. 'Well, as I
was saying our respected client is much troubled.'

'Much troubled', echoed the client.

'Much troubled', went on the solicitor. 'You see he invented the Tank.'

'He what?' I could hardly believe my ears.

'He invented the Tank—you know, the crawling vehicle
which played such a part in recent wars.'

'Oh, I know what a tank is, but are you saying Mr Hooter
invented it? I thought it had been invented ages ago.'

'It was ages ago that I invented it,' the client observed
politely.

'He got the idea', the solicitor remarked, 'from a cater-
pillar.'

I was now convinced that I was in the company of two raving lunatics. Harmless maybe, but that remained to be seen. No wonder they were being followed—no doubt by warders.

'I see', I said, determined to humour them. 'Very ingenious.'

'Ingenious—the very word I used', said the solicitor.

'An apt and inspired description it I may say so.'

What a pity, I thought, that a solicitor who had been so richly impressed by me should be a temporary refugee from an asylum, in no position to give me further work.

The solicitor bent down and withdrew from his brief case the most enormous file of papers. 'Now the point is', he said, 'that the War Office and His Majesty's Government have absolutely refused to entertain the claim. I have the file of correspondence here.' He patted it. 'I need only refer to the last letter', he said. 'The one in reply to me after I came on the scene last month.'

I was relieved. 'What does it say?' I asked.

'They have the impertinence—the gross impertinence—to say that they have nothing to add to their previous letters and that the correspondence must now cease'.

I saw their point.

'Never in sixty-four years as a solicitor, Mr Comyn, have I been treated thus.'

I nodded sympathetically.

'Told after my very first letter that the correspondence must cease. Such impertinence I have never heard. I have naturally reported the matter.'

'To whom?' I was genuinely curious.

'To the Prime Minister, of course—and to the Leader of the Opposition.'

'Of course.'

'Well, there it is,' said the solicitor, obviously outraged, but trying to keep it in check out of a sense of duty to his client. 'The point is what do we do now?'

I had not the faintest idea, beyond the obvious one—
which would naturally be most unpopular—of letting the
whole thing drop. I pursed my lips and looked wise. I
thought hard. At last the Oracle spoke. 'Mr Hooter', I
asked 'are you married?'

'I was, but she has departed'. This was not surprising
until he added, 'She has been long deceased'.

I found great attraction in the way these old-world
gentlemen spoke.

'I'm sorry,' I said.

'I don't think I am', Mr Hooter unexpectedly replied;
'she was inclined to be tiresome.'

'Have you any children?'

'None.'

'Any near relatives?'

'Neither near nor far. I am alone in the world.'

'Where do you live?' This was a clever one, designed to
test the Asylum theory.

'He lives', said the solicitor, 'beside me on an island in
the River Thames.'

This nearly put me beyond speech altogether.

'Are there islands on the Thames?' I asked.

'Indeed,' said the solicitor. 'Habited and uninhabited.'

I had to bite my tongue to stop me asking on which
kind they lived.

'It was on that very island', remarked the solicitor
proudly, 'that this great idea first occurred to Mr Hooter.'
He paused. 'There will be a plaque there some day.'

'You could put one up yourself,' I observed, feeling
that I must say something constructive.

'I intend to.' The reply came not from the solicitor to
whom the observation was addressed, but from the client.

'Is it', asked the solicitor, 'significant to your mind, Mr
Comyn, that our client is bereft of all living relatives?'

'Very.'

'Pray why?'

'Because', I said, 'it solves the whole matter.'

They looked at me with great surprise.

'There is of course', I went on, 'no question of Mr Hooter wanting any money for this invention.'

Now they thought I was mad.

'And that being the case', I said without waiting for the answer, 'the solution is plain.'

'Yes?'

'Mr Hooter will leave his invention to the nation.'

They looked at me and then looked at each other.

'And you', I said turning to the solicitor, 'will draft the will. And be the executor.'

A faint—very faint—smile returned to the solicitor's face. 'It will need thinking about', they said as they left— never to return.

'What's the Position, Now?'

I was walking back to chambers from court one evening about half past four, pleased that for once there would be no consultation waiting. 'I can have a bit of a nap', I said to Clement, my clerk. 'Or you can get some of those outstanding papers done', he replied unkindly. 'I can do both', I said witheringly. 'You're never any good after you've been asleep', he said, having the last word as usual.

We arrived back to chambers to be greeted by a junior clerk saying to me, 'They're in your room.' I turned to Clement and said, 'But I haven't got a con.' He was unsympathetic. 'Apparently you have now', he said.

I went disconsolately to my room. A solicitor's clerk and a lay client, neither of whom I recognised, were on their feet when I came in. We shook hands.

Seated behind my desk I waited for the solicitor's clerk to start, but nothing came. So to start the ball rolling I said tentatively, 'Well, what's the position now?' He coughed nervously and said, 'Nothing really has happened since that letter you drafted nine months ago.' 'Is it nine months?' I said playing for time; 'how the months have passed' 'Nine months last Tuesday', he replied morosely.

'Can I have a look at it again', I said eyeing his file.

He made no effort to pass me the file. 'It was just threatening proceedings', he said.

'What was the reply?'

'There was no reply at all', he said.

'Did nothing happen?'

'Nothing at all.'

I had to get the file to see if there was any way at all to recapture to my memory this elusive matter. I usually have a very good memory for recapturing ('retrieving' is I think the word)

'Could I just glance through the file?' I asked politely. 'Just to refresh my memory on a few points.'

Apparently reluctant, the clerk passed over the file and I whizzed through it. A claim for damage to a car, but not in a road accident. Insurers were on the scene and were dragging their feet.

I was about to say, 'Issue a writ tomorrow' when my senior clerk came in and said 'Mr Hugh Bennett is ready to see the clients now', as if I were a sort of waiting room or pre-operative chamber. Then with all the skill of a barrister's clerk, he had the clients on their feet and nearly at the door. A noble thing happened at that stage. The lay client, who had not uttered a word, turned, shook my hand and said, 'Thank you.'

I wandered into the chamber room, leant near to the junior clerk and said 'Take eight years notice.'

An Enjoyable Consultation

I was to have a consultation with some Greek Cypriot lay clients one afternoon about a commercial matter in which they wished to sue some Turkish Cypriots. The papers in the case were bulky and I had managed to read little more than half of them before the consultation.

I confessed this frankly to the clients, who were completely understanding. 'Not to worry', said their head man. 'The story is simple. Both sides, we are all a bunch of crooks, but they are bigger crooks than we are.' It turned out to be a brilliant and accurate summing up of the case.

Roger Bannister's Mile

Sir Charles Russell and Cyril Russell of Charles Russell and Company are close friends of mine. Cyril it was who brought me a remarkable lay client. We were able to sort out his troubles quite quickly and fairly easily.

As the consultation was ending I congratulated him on the fame he had achieved (and though I did not mention it, dwelling on the money he must have made) by producing and speedily selling worldwide a full telerecording of Roger Bannister's historic under-four-minute mile. I had seen the film three times and it was superb; it gave not only the whole race but also a long elaborate pre-race 'build up' from Iffley Road, Oxford, the university track upon which Roger Bannister was about to make sporting history; if I'm not too Irish in saying so, a piece of history which everyone had been looking forward to for a long time.

'You're a wonderful man', I said, 'how on earth did you get it?'

He smiled broadly. 'Quite easy really, Mr Comyn,' he said.

'I knew of course that breaking the four-minute mile would be history with a big H. So, about two years before the big race, with the help of my staff I picked out four names throughout the world as being the chaps likely to pull this off. Then I simply had every single mile race that each chap ran filmed from start to finish, with elaborate prerace build-up, direct from the track. So—quite easy you see.'

We marvelled and redoubled our congratulation. That man really deserved his success.

There is, however, a sad postscript to the story. Little though I had done for the client he sent me a handsome present, a lovely diamond and pearl-studded waistcoat chain. I treasured it, I occasionally wore it, but it was stolen from me a couple of years later.

Margaret, Duchess of Argyll

That famous and fascinating character was a client of Sir Charles Russell and when she was in dispute with her step-mother about her father's will he briefed me. We were, I am glad to say, successful.

On another occasion Cyril Russell briefed me for the Duchess of Rutland, the Duchess of Argyll's daughter. That case, too, was successful.

The Duchess of Argyll's father, Mr Whigham, was, I believe, very proud of having both a daughter and a grand-daughter duchesses.

Letters

Cyril Russell could write the most politely offensive letters to the other side when the occasion demanded. This used to bring out the worst (? the best) in me, when drafting letters for him in an effort to match his correspondence. We used to tone down each other's letters—and quite often were successful. One case I remember is where we got our client reinstated by his professional body after a barrage of increasingly nasty letters from us.

9

The AA Solicitor and a Cat and a Stone

I FIRST CAME UPON THE PHENOMENON of the AA (Automobile Association) solicitor at Bow Street Magistrate's Court one morning about 1950.

Of, say, sixty motoring cases, he was appearing in, say, forty-five, for members of the AA who were pleading guilty to a variety of minor offences and were not themselves present in court. It was part, a useful part, of the AA service to its members.

Everything short was tried in batches there. A batch of soliciting cases (I had had two), a batch of drunk and disorderlies, a batch of unopposed applications, now a batch of motoring offences. Cases were rolling off the production line at speed. I had a contested assault case due for hearing later, and though never an admirer of great speed in court, and finding a magistrate's boast that he had 'got through' 100 cases that morning nasty, I welcomed speed here. I actually had another case, elsewhere, at Ilford, in the afternoon.

'*RAMSBOTTOM*, speeding', the clerk of the court would call out. 'I appear for Mrs Ramsbottom', the AA solicitor would say.

'54 miles an hour in Aldwych, lunch-time', the prosecuting solicitor would say; 'no previous.' Then the AA solicitor, flipping through his large bundle of papers, would say, 'She's very sorry. Aldwych surprisingly free of traffic at that time. She was in a hurry to meet her husband in Holborn for lunch. Didn't realise she was doing

as much as fifty-four miles an hour. Driving a brand new
Morris. Apologies. Seventeen years driving. No accidents.
Clear licence. Nobody put at risk here.' Then the stipen-
diary magistrate spoke: 'Fined £24, seven days. Licence
endorsed. Costs' (It seemed, roughly speaking, £1 a mile
for every mile over thirty m.p.h).

Everybody jotted down the result.

Then the case of *Higgins* was called. 'In that too, sir',
said the AA solicitor, flipping through his papers. The prosecuting solicitor said, 'Christmas Eve. Strand, Fleet Street
end. No vehicle licence showing, No Insurance; two days
out'. 'No insurance always serious', observed the magistrate.
Then the AA solicitor: 'A twenty-seven year old reporter
with the Express. Unmarried. . .'. (I enjoyed that. Its
relevance must have been great.) 'He didn't realise he had
no vehicle disc showing. He had a valid one. It must have
fallen down and got lost. He has a replacement one now.'
'What about No Insurance?' enquired the magistrate, 'I
always take a serious view of that. If there was an accident,
you know.' 'He was very busy at the time. He overlooked
it. Very sorry. I've been through to the insurance company, the Sun Alliance, and they tell me that they'd have
covered him, up to fourteen days. He took out a full
year's insurance immediately afterward No record. Clear
licence.' The magistrate was much mollified but felt obliged
to say something more about no insurance. 'Very careless
for a man in your client's position', he said (I almost
laughed; I'm afraid I laugh easily: ' a man in your client's
position', sounded as if he was the editor of the *Express* or
the *Standard* or something like that). 'I'm glad the insurers
would have had him covered. But Christmas Eve, you
know, a lot of people about. . .'. (I nearly laughed again:
so that was the relevance of Christmas.) 'There might
have been an accident. I always take a serious view of No
Insurance.' (Quite right of course, I said to myself, but
hasn't he already made that abundantly clear? This case is
taking an inordinate length of time.) 'Very well', said the

magistrate; 'in all the circumstances I can take a lenient
view. No disc—fined five shillings. No Insurance. Only
two days and had been covered.' (I was waiting for him to
say once again that it was nevertheless serious, but he
didn't.) 'Lenient view', he said. 'Very lenient view. Fine
ten shillings. Both fines seven days.' Then he added something which to me seemed wrong; I'd look it up when
I got back to chambers: 'Needn't endorse here', he said,
adding 'costs fixed at five guineas'. 'Thank you, sir', everyone said.

Perhaps things would get a move on now. My case
would last about half an hour and I had to get right across
London to Ilford for my case in the afternoon, marked
'six guineas', plus, of course, clerk's fee (the guineas and
the clerk's fee are now abolished). I was getting a bit
worried about time. I always worry about time—on everything. I went through life at the Bar thinking that 'two
o'clock' meant two o'clock, and I must be there at ten to
two to see the client.

I was usually still there, not yet reached, at half past
four. I wish I'd been like David Moylan or Jim Hale of
chambers, or my old Western Circuit golf and bridge
partner, Guy Willett (grandson of the inventor of Summer
Time), all of whom got to court in leisurely, unworried
fashion at 10.29 or 2.05 and invariably found that all was
well. I always worried too about papers which were marked
'Urgent'. I thought they always meant 'Urgent'. The
nicer phrase 'Despatch Will Oblige' did not sound half so
Urgent. Anyway all through my time at the Bar I looked
at every new brief or set of instructions which came in,
that same night without fail. Partly curiosity, but partly
relief at still being sent work.

Then an absolutely delicious thing happened in the AA
solicitor case at Bow Street business. The case of, say, *Beach,*
Emily Gertrude, was called. The AA solicitor obviously
thought it was one of his and went through his file. First
time round he couldn't find it. So he began another

search. The already much flipped-through file fell apart in his hands; a large, ugly-looking staple with spikes, reared its head—and he stubbed his finger on it. 'Ouch', he cried , jumping to his feet, 'Ouch', and bending in half put his injured hand between his legs.

'Are you alright, Mr Amery?' (that was not in fact his name), enquired the magistrate solicitously.

'I've stubbed my finger on that bloody thing, sir', said the the AA solicitor, pointing with a finger of the other hand at the offending, now scattered, file.

'I'm sorry, Mr Amery. I see it's bleeding. Shall I send for the Matron?'

Mr Amery's prosecuting friend moved over to him and put an arm round him. Mr Amery took out a large silk handkerchief and wound it round and round the wounded finger.

'No need, thank you, sir,' he said gallantly. 'It'll be alright in a minute. It's shock really. I wasn't expecting it. Bloody thing.'

Then I really dissolved into laughter. Cruel and unsympathetic, I know, but I couldn't help it. I never can help it. I'd have to go out of court. I needed a Sweet Afton anyway.

As I crept along counsel's bench I bowed to the magistrate and he bowed back to me. As I was leaving the court I heard the brave AA solicitor, a true professional doing his duty come what may, say to the magistrate respectfully, ruefully, 'So sorry, sir. I don't think I'm in this case after all.'

Paroxysms of laughter now overcame me and I rolled out into the crowded corridor, giving a nod to the police office at the door of the court, whom I knew well, who looked astonished at this usually staid but sometimes leg-pulling, always smoking when not in court, young Irish counsel. What in Heaven's name had been happening in court, he was obviously asking himself. What has young 'Mr Cunningham' been up to now?

I recovered. My assault case came on soon. I did it badly. We lost. We were fined £25 and costs. Perhaps nobody could have won it. The client was bad too. Another firm of valuable solicitors down the drain. (Happily no.)

I got to Ilford in good time for my other case. I even had time for a coffee and a sandwich at a 'Pull Up for Car Men', a few yards across the road from the magistrates' court. I always like to have my court in full sight before I relax. That is why I was not good at travelling down to, say, Southampton, early in the morning for a 10.30 a.m. case. I used to travel down the night before and stay at a hotel near the court. 'Why don't you go by sleeper, James?' asked Kenneth Willcock (now His Honour Judge Willcock QC) of chambers on one occasion.

I won the Ilford case. Well, nearly won it. Found Guilty but only Bound Over.

All the way back from Ilford by train to chambers I was looking forward to telling the boys in chambers at tea-time—Robin Dunn, Roger Gray, Roger Ormrod, David Moylan, Harry Phillimore (fresh from some triumph in the Court of Appeal, no doubt), and my friends Paul Wrightson and Patrick Back—all about the AA solicitor.

Letting the Cat out of the Bag

At Lambeth County Court before Judge Clothier QC, I was appearing for landlords who were seeking to evict from her flat a middle-aged lady. On one of the grounds permitted by the Rent Acts—that she was guilty of 'nuisance and annoyance'.

My opponent was a regular opponent and old friend, Alan Campbell, now Lord Campbell of Alloway QC. He it was who appealed me successfully in the leading case of *Solle v. Butcher*.

Nothing unusual occurred during my case and I thought that with the aid of adjoining tenants we had prepared a straight case of 'nuisance and annoyance'.

Then Alan Campbell called his client. She looked sad and demure and attributed all the trouble to her neighbours not liking her and wanting to get rid of her at all costs. It was evident that Judge Clothier was taking a liking to her and being sympathetic towards her.

I rose to cross-examine and said, 'Madam', whereupon she bent down in the witnessbox, rustled in a bag and produced a dead cat, which she threw at me. It hit me on the chest, but I remained upright.

Then Judge Clothier uttered these immortal words: 'Madam, if you do that again I'll commit you.'

The case was won, and I count it as a remarkable example of cross-examination.

'A Stone's Throw from the Sea'

Of all my cases the one I am proudest of having won is *Steadman v S. Tours* (1946), which entailed that a person can get damages from tour operators for 'a spoilt holiday'.

It was all fairly new territory just after the 1939–1945 war. My clients, husband and wife, had saved up for a foreign holiday with S. Tours, an enterprise later to be very famous.

My nice couple said that they had not got what they had been promised, it turned out to be an awful holiday, in horrid accommodation. They sued for damages for breach of contract, to include 'compensation' for a thoroughly spoilt holiday.

We lost in the county court. The county court judge held *inter alia* that there was no such thing in law as damages for a spoilt holiday. We went to the Court of Appeal. I was burning with a sense of injustice on behalf of my clients. I got off to an awkward start before the Lord Justices—one often does, but it can come right in the end (of course quite often it just doesn't). I described to their Lordships the accommodation promised and the accommodation actually provided. There had been one good phrase in the brochure which I had fastened on, but which the county court judge had pooh-pooed; it said that the hotel was 'within a stone's throw of the sea'.

I do not suppose that their Lordships had ever heard of 'a package holiday' before, much less been on one. They began to show a bit of curiosity, a bit of interest, a bit of life. I said that it was a little hard that, with the wretched room and the wretched food they had got, my poor clients had had to walk nearly a mile to get to the sea.

The Master of the Rolls, Sir Raymond (later Lord) Evershed—he had been, as a chancery man, the youngest man ever to be appointed a KC, at the age of 33—leant back in his chair and with a smile eyed this young, earnest, rather outspoken, rather assured young Irishman who was appearing for the appellants. In 'cloistered chancery' he did not meet many like him.

'I suppose, Mr Comyn, you'd say that on these admitted facts, even Hercules in his heyday could not have got a pebble to the sea from this hotel.'

'Even if he was standing on the roof,' interjected his colleague on the right.

'Yes, My Lord, Yes, My Lord, That's just what I would say, but Your Lordship puts it so much better than I have.'

'I don't know about that', said the Master of the Rolls nicely.

All their Lordships evidently liked the idea of Hercules, and they developed it.

'How far', asked the Master of the Rolls of me, 'how far do you suppose that Hercules in his heyday could have thrown a stone—a reasonably sized stone—from this hotel?' He and his colleagues were smilingly awaiting my reply.

It would appear to be a wholly new (but splendid) concept, but the precise question took me by surprise.

'I suppose', I said, 'about half way up the High Street.'

'Oh, I don't know,' said the MR, 'I don't think he'd have managed even as far as that.'

Within a few minutes it began to dawn on me that I was winning; in the only two cases I had brought from the county court to the Court of Appeal, I had lost hopelessly.

So I 'stoked' the idea of Hercules. I said that Hercules to get any distance at all would have needed to have been well fed, which he wouldn't be at this hotel.

'And Guinness for strength,' remarked the third Lord Justice.

'Anyway', said the Master eventually, 'you'd say, Mr Comyn, that even Hercules in his heyday' (I loved, their Lordships loved, 'Hercules in his heyday') 'could have been throwing stones, reasonably sized stones, all day and wouldn't have been anywhere near the sea, even if the tide was in?'

'Yes, Yes, Yes, My Lord.'

We won hands down.

Well done, Hercules.

10

Air Affairs

BALPA

FOR MANY YEARS WHEN I WAS a junior counsel I regularly acted as counsel for the British Airline Pilots' Association (never alas for the air-hostesses or for Aer Lingus pilots).

I was instructed by the late Evan Davies of Evan Davies and Company of Buckingham Gate (whose brother and partner Ninian was also a professional client of mine). They had a most admirable managing clerk, James Hyde, who was a great friend of my very, very great friend, my clerk, Clement. James Hyde was one of the most efficient (and best dressed and best mannered) managing clerks I have ever met.

For a large part of the period we had the benefit of Dennis Follows as the indefatigable secretary of BALPA. Then he went to the Football League. It was a particular pleasure when he was knighted.

BALPA and their members were frequently at odds with BEA (British European Airways) and BOAC (British Overseas Airways Corporation), now amalgamated as British Airways, over a variety of things—pay, allowances, hours of duty, conditions of service, even meals. You could hardly credit it but I spent no less than three days before an industrial tribunal, which sat somewhere near the Houses of Parliament, arguing for better meals for the air crew on the Barcelona run. We got them, having been made to fight all the way. I was, I remember, very biased; but how BEA in particular continued to run an airline in the light of their attitude to their flying crews I will never understand.

It was hard but entertaining work acting for BALPA. Hardly a week passed without my being called upon to advise them about something or to represent them before some court or tribunal.

Happily we managed to get many of their disputes with their employers ironed out and settled without having to go to any court. I remember once the very tired crew who had just completed, a few hours before, an arduous tour of transatlantic duty assembling in my chambers in the Temple to deal with an important and urgent BOAC 'directive'. Happily we managed to get it sorted out too, but only after, and during a consultation which went on in my chambers from 5 p.m. until nearly midnight. I was completely exhausted by then. What 'the boys' must have felt like I cannot imagine.

There was immense variety about the work. One member I had to defend twice in respect of the same matter. He was a very senior BOAC pilot. Off-duty, and contrary to his contract with BOAC, he used to do some private commercial flying on his own account. He was a very skilled pilot, but on one occasion he undoubtedly did jeopardise the safety of an airliner (a Russian one at that) coming in to land at Gatwick. He was flying a wrong course and flying too low and too fast. Happily a potentially terrible disaster was averted—by a matter of seconds and a matter of feet.

He was charged at the local court with a series of offences arising out of this. We pleaded Guilty to some and had pleas of Not Guilty to the remainder accepted—after some hard bargaining—by a very decent prosecution. He was fined a total of something like £3,000. But the Bench, lay magistrates, liked and admired him (you could not help doing so) and sympathised with him for a most untypical error. They expressed the hope that his employers would not 'ground him' or punish him too severely. I then appeared for him before a disciplinary committee of the employers, and in this instance they were charitable and

decided only on a severe reprimand. He flew again for
them almost immediately and there was never any more
trouble. Of course, they needed him; probably more than
he needed them. But under his contract they could have
summarily dismissed him and if they had done there was
nothing we could do about it. There would be no success
(indeed abject failure) if we went to court about it.

The work involved defending pilots and crew members on
various minor, criminal charges; with mixed results. And
advising and acting for members in various kinds of civil
claims. On this BALPA and I had a better record than in
petty crime. We did not of course act in respect of purely
personal crime matters but our 'union protection' did ex-
tend to road traffic accident claims and to defending (or
mitigating in respect of) charges of motoring offences.

There were a few major air disaster inquests and enquiries.
One concerned an accident at or rather near Blackbushe in
Hampshire. Another concerned a disaster at Southall in
Middlesex. In the course of the inquest in respect of the
latter I happened, I remember (I will never forget), to
make a most unfortunate observation. Two of my learned
colleagues, representing other interests, unfortunately got
into a running quarrel with the excessively quarrelsome
and tiresome coroner. I tried many times to help but got
rebuffed. Finally I stood up and said, 'May I once again,
sir, try to pour burning oil on troubled waters.' I still
shiver when I think of the terrible lapse of language which
made me say 'burning oil'. A deadly hush fell over the
whole court. Even the press men shuddered.

It was at that inquest that one of the counsel whom the
coroner was gunning for, Roy Fox Andrews QC, made a
splendid and silencing retort to him.

'Are you accusing me of bias—unfairness?' demanded
the coroner.

Roy Fox Andrews delayed his reply: then suddenly slowly
and solemnly: '*Quod scripsi scripsi*', which roughly means

(the coroner certainly did not understand it or its source) 'What I have said I have said.'

There were fortunately funny, or near funny episodes too. Funny and sad. Once I had to defend a very capable and usually dependable BEA pilot on a disciplinary charge which, stripped of its jargon, means 'unfortunate practical joking'. He was forever practising practical jokes, on board and on land, and on everyone—usually quite harmless and readily understood and 'forgiven' by all concerned. However, on this occasion it was alleged and admitted that he had gone 'beyond the bounds'. Lolling comfortably in the front seat of an aircraft bound, I think, for Hamburg, and having disguised his official status, when the 'plane was late in starting off he suddenly got up, took off his jacket and shouted, so that all in the aircraft would hear, 'Well, if nobody's going to get this bloody thing off the ground I'd better have a crack at it myself', and he went towards, and into, the crew quarters.

We had no defence; just mitigation. But it failed. He had 'japed' once too often. He was summarily dismissed.

One heard splendid, thankfully apocryphal, stories from 'the boys'. I will just mention two, of hundreds. The first concerns an alleged (imaginary) incident when the crew of a modern jet about to take off for Bombay from Heathrow were suddenly smitten with food poisoning. The passengers were told and were assured that happily a competent replacement crew were to hand. Five minutes later the replacement crew entered the aircraft and went through (and this shows why the story happily cannot be literally true), walked down the aisle between the passengers. The new captain came to the middle of the aircraft. He stopped, and then, pointing to both sides of the wings, said audibly to his crew, 'Goodness gracious me; no propellers. What shall we do?' And went on his way plus new crew to the crew deck.

The other apocryphal story concerns another airline.

Approaching London on a flight from, say, Dakar, dense fog was encountered. It was said to be impenetrable and the aircraft was diverted (so the story went) to Cambridge Airport. The captain announced this to the passengers and told them there was nothing to worry about. About a quarter of an hour later a worried looking second officer emerged from the flight deck and at the top of his voice enquired, 'Does anybody here know Cambridge?' An elderly gentleman a few rows down got up and said, 'Well actually I do, I was up at King's for three years.'

'Oh good,' said the second officer, 'just you come up here with me, sir. Perhaps you'd be able to identify Cambridge from the air.'

I personally had several experiences aboard aircraft. For many years I used to fly to and from Heathrow to Ireland virtually every weekend. I flew the Atlantic on legal business (to advise Bristol Myers on pharmaceutical legal matters). I went to Gibraltar on a case. I flew to Hong Kong on cases.

Once I was, incredibly, the only passenger on the return journey from Dublin.

Unfortunately I got 'nervy' (I had never grown wholly fearless when airborne). I kept seeing headlines saying, 'Air Disaster at Heathrow. Fortunately only one passenger killed.'

On another occasion I heard one of the best remarks I ever heard. We were approaching London from Dublin. It was very foggy. The pilot gingerly and cleverly brought the aircraft down, but we were, as I could see, crossing the flare path. He quickly pulled her up and a few seconds later announced, splendid man, 'Ladies and gentlemen, I've just been down to have a look for myself. It's not too good but we'll make it next time.' Thank God we did. As we disembarked I heard a husband say to his wife, 'I could just see tomorrow's papers' headlines.' She put an affectionate hand on his arm and said, 'I'm afraid, darling, I didn't think we'd live to see tomorrow's papers.'

Then there was another occasion when, flying from London to Dublin, there was thick fog at Dublin. The captain announced he would have to divert to Shannon. This greatly distressed the passenger sitting beside me. He called an Aer Lingus hostess (my fellow-countrywomen do look attractive in their uniforms). He told her he was disturbed because his wife was dying in a Dublin hospital and he had been urgently summoned to be with her. Diversion to Shannon might mean he was too late. She said that she would have a word with the captain. And she did. A few moments later the captain said, 'Ladies and gentlemen, I will try to land at Dublin—if it is at all safe to do so. But if not, you'll understand I'll have to come up again and go on to Shannon.'

As BALPA counsel I of course knew a lot about aircraft and about problems and risk. The captain made a most beautiful and delicate descent and run-in. He 'crept' in over Dublin Bay and across the city, 'inching' his way down. Then, a few minutes later, light as a feather he made a tentative touchdown at Dublin Airport. At first tentative, then progressively more lively, it was a quite superb touchdown and he throttled back violently and brought the craft to a stop very quickly. The passengers gave him a standing ovation. I subsequently wrote to the Top Man at Dublin Airport congratulating the pilot most heartily, and got a gracious reply. I do wish I could remember his name.

But meantime my BALPA 'boys'. We went on our way mostly merrily and quite often with success or large measure of success. Some dismal failures.

Then came Captain Thain.

Captain Thain—1958

I appeared for Captain Thain, in the following circumstances. Captain Thain was an experienced and skilful pilot just aged thirty seven when, on 6 February 1958, he was captain in charge and co-pilot of a BEA Elizabethan aircraft which was on special charter to Manchester United Football Club. United had had a European Cup fixture at Belgrade against Red Star and were returning in foul weather, when, after a fuel stop at Munich, the plane crashed on take-off (the co-pilot, Captain Rayment, crying out as on the tape, 'Christ, we won't make it'). Twenty-three of the passengers, a little under half the total, were killed, and this included eight of the team.

The aircraft encountered bad weather flying into Munich, and there was a good deal of snow on the ground. The runway had some snow, slush and water, but there was no special difficulty in landing. At about 3.19 p.m. the aircraft made to take off, but before reaching the critical point the take-off was abandoned. A second take-off was then attempted, but was similarly abandoned. After an interval, the third take-off was started at four minutes to four and it was that which ended in disaster, the aircraft failing to become airborne by the end of the runway, crossing a small road and ploughing into a house.

One of the points raised at the various inquiries was about there having been a third take-off. It may sound ominous in retrospect, but unless the whole operation were to be abandoned there would have had to be a numerically third attempt whenever it took place—for example, even if delayed overnight.

The cause of the crash and whether Captain Thain was to blame occupied the attention of a German committee of justice, which was re-convened three times, and two British inquiries.

Captain Thain started with many disadvantages, but two became particularly prominent; one, that in the stopover at Munich he had not examined the wings for icing; two, that contrary to a BEA ruling (but not under any other rules) he was sitting in the wrong seat, the right-hand seat, when, as the person in command, he should have been in the left-hand seat. The seating point earned him the blame of BEA and their unhelpfulness to him in his trials. They, in fact, based their eventual dismissal of him on it.

The German inquiry was long and critical. It found the cause of the crash to have been ice on the wings and blamed Captain Thain squarely but not, as it happens, fairly. Despite additional evidence and reasoned arguments by Captain Thain and his colleagues and experts, they refused on three subsequent occasions to alter or modify their findings in any way at all. Captain Thain's contention was that it was nothing to do with icing, that the crash was solely due to slush on the runway and that the incident had revealed how inadequate the knowledge had been of the effect of slush. For the first time ever there was a strong focusing of attention on the effect of slush—its retarding force counteracting and contradicting the speed of the aircraft and throwing out a pilot's instruments and decisions.

The British Government need not have held any type of public inquiry because the crash took place abroad. But they did and appointed to head it a brilliant and distinguished barrister Mr E.S. Fay QC, sitting with two experts, Professor A.R. Collard and Captain R.P. Wigley. Captain Thain based his case on the fact that the evidence showed nothing of ice on the wings at the time of take-offs and that slush and only slush was the cause, nobody realizing that slush of the relatively small quantity (small, but spread, and altering in its texture) could cause what happened on these three occasions. The depth of the slush varied between one and one and a half inches.

The First Fay Report (because he headed a second inquiry) found that it must be accepted from the German commission that there was ice on the wings, though not established as the German 5mm and may have been substantially less, and that they were 'unable to make any useful deduction as to the presence of ice or the degree of slush drag'. On three specific questions which they were asked, they cleared Captain Thain on two—checking the state of the runway and taking proper steps to find out the cause of the two earlier difficulties—but found him to blame for 'a serious error' in not examining the wings before the third attempt.

On the question of ice Captain Thain had three points to make: there was no evidence of any ice until long after the crash; he exercised the judgment of a careful captain; and the crash, he asserted, was nothing to do with ice anyway but all due to slush, and nobody suggested that he should have appreciated that slush of the kind and extent present there should have put him off taking off.

Captain Thain was fortunate in having as a sympathizer the prime minister, Mr Harold Wilson. At a Manchester United dinner he said in as many words that 'the captain of the aircraft had been unfairly treated ever since', and he based himself on researches about slush which had taken place at Farnborough. The British inquiry was re-opened, or, more property stated, a fresh inquiry was set up, again with Mr Fay as chairman, again with Professor Collard but this time with, as a third member, Captain Jeffrey. John May QC (later Lord Justice May) represented Captain Thain on this second Fay inquiry.

The Second Fay Inquiry came out with its conclusion. It did not eliminate ice or frozen snow on the wings. 'The outer wings. . . on its final run may or may not have carried a thin deposit. . .' but it would have been very thin. The effective cause of the accident was slush drag. 'Our considered view, therefore, is that the cause of the accident was slush on the runway. Whether wing icing was also a cause, we cannot say. It is possible but unlikely.' The criticism of Captain Thain for not examining the wings for ice remained. Both he and Captain Rayment were cleared of any blame in handling the aircraft.

The BA rule about the left-hand and right-hand seats registered as a proper matter to raise but as being of no importance at all in the case. The tribunal indeed criticized the rule, saying that Captain Rayment was obviously happier and was likely to have been more efficient in the seat to which he was accustomed.

Captain Thain never did any further professional flying. He and his wife (a scientist who was of tremendous help to him and to us on 'slush' experiments) took to chicken farming in Buckinghamshire—not far from Heathrow. He died a few years ago. His was a personal tragedy. He became a sad man, but it is as a brave man and brilliant pilot and captain that he should be remembered, the man who established the full and real dangers of slush. A man who was vindicated but still had attached to his name a niggling doubt about wing inspection and the absurdity of seating.

11

Alfie Hinds and Ors

Alfie Hinds

ALFIE HINDS—LITIGANT EXTRAORDINARY and Gaol Escaper Incomparable!

I first met this extraordinary and splendid man when the Isle of Wight solicitor Percy Rolfe and Miss Cawes briefed me as QC in the celebrated case Alfie Hinds took against ex-Detective Chief-Superintendent Sparks, for libel in 1964. The junior was an old friend of mine, Bryan Anns. He was later a QC and died tragically in a swimming-pool accident when out in the Far East, doing a case.

I was the third choice of leading counsel. The first was Gerald Gardiner QC—but he became Lord Chancellor! The second was Kenneth Mynett QC (now Judge Mynett QC) but shortly before the trial he had to return the brief.

It was my luck. I was a relatively new QC and this was an important case, although the odds seemed all against us.

Alfie Hinds has told his whole fascinating story in a non-ghosted book called *Contempt of Court*—meaning his contempt for courts generally. The only legal characters who emerge 'unscathed' from it—indeed praised—are myself, Bryan Anns, Percy Rolfe, and the QC who opposed us in the libel action, and who cross-examined Alfie Hinds for five days, Desmond Ackner QC (now, a law lord, Lord Ackner). Alfie Hinds came to admire him greatly, as I always did.

The book was published (certainly to my surprise) by The Bodley Head. I am biased, but it really is a good book. A quite extraordinary true, factual story.

Put shortly, the Alfie Hinds' case arose in this way. The famous Tottenham Court Road store, Maples, was robbed of over £38,000 of money and jewellery on Thursday evening, 24 September 1953.

Detective Chief-Superintendent Sparks of Scotland Yard was put in charge of the case. He had as assistants Detective Constables Budd and Tiddy. It proved to be 'a gelly job'. A safe at Maples had been blown open. The robbers had been admitted to Maples by two 'insiders'. Soon Sparks and his team picked up two of the men involved— 'insiders' George Williams, a fireman employed on the premises, and James Gridley, night security superintendent.

They then soon afterwards caught two other men, William Nicholls and Frank Martin.

All four of these pleaded Guilty at the subsequent trial before the Lord Chief Justice, Lord Goddard, at the Old Bailey.

There was, beyond question, a fifth man involved. And Sparks and his men decided it was Alfie Hinds, a five foot ten, wiry, distinctive looking cockney, who 'had had it hard', had convictions for pretty petty crimes (nothing remotely like this) and was in a demolition business with his brother (which Sparks maintained was 'a blind').

Alfie Hinds was at the time living with 'Peg' (now his wife) and their family at a bungalow at Wraysbury, by the river near Staines. On the Sunday following the robbery Sparks and his team descended upon Alfie Hinds at his bungalow. They found there a man named Porter, an associate of Nicholls. They now had, they thought, a second important thing on Hinds, because there was a dispute (he never denied it) that on the Monday evening before the robbery—when a rehearsal of the robbery took place at Maples—he was within half a mile of Maples, in the company of Porter and Nicholls. He—and they—said it was nothing to do with the robbery but was solely for the purpose of selling him a carpet. They had intended to steal the carpet from Maples, a famous place for carpets, but the carpet deal did not come off. Hinds did not know that the carpet was to be stolen.

The detective superintendent and his team were convinced that Alfie Hinds was the leader of the robbery gang, was present at Maples on rehearsal evening, took part in the robbery and was the man who 'blew' the safe. Hinds most vigorously denied having had any part whatsoever in the robbery. In that denial he has all through and ever since violently persisted.

Gridley, who co-operated with the police from the start, presumably hoping for leniency, identified Hinds as being there and being the ring leader. Gridley was represented by David Napley. In addition, it was claimed by Sparks, and subsequently the prosecution, that incriminating 'debris dust' from the 'timber wadding' of the safe was found in the turn-ups of Hind's trousers. Sparks and Tiddy also claimed that the Sunday at the bungalow Alfie Hind's 'verballed' admissions. And Budd claimed the same at the police station in London. He was arrested and charged with the robbery. He was the only one of the five who pleaded Not Guilty.

Now, defended by a last-minute QC and junior instructed by James H. Fellowers, a well known East End solicitor, the QC was given only a quarter of an hour to see him. Hinds came up at Court No. 1 at the Old Bailey before that formidable figure, Lord Chief Justice Goddard.

'Doggie' Goddard, a famous burly tough Lord Chief (who had in fact once been an athletic 'blue' at Oxford, though you could hardly imagine it) was particularly 'hot' on violent crime. He was a great man, and a great Lord Chief. Let there be no doubt about that. He was ninety five per cent of the time dead right. But when he was wrong, did he go wrong!

His big fault was that he 'jumped' quickly in a case (it is said that Mr Justice—Jimmy—Cassels once said to him as they went into court to take their seats in the Court of Criminal Appeal, 'Don't dismiss the first three appeals, Rayner, before giving me a chance to sit down').

Everything that possibly could go wrong went wrong at the Hind's trial. It was, from first to last, an absolute disgrace—a severe blot on British justice and on the otherwise deservedly high reputation of the Lord Chief and Sparks.

Hinds was quickly—much, much, too quickly—convicted. Sparks gave him an appalling 'character', and he and the Lord Chief were convinced that Alfie Hinds was an exceedingly dangerous criminal, the leader of 'the gelly boys'. But Sparks had never before encountered Hinds and had no excuse for most of what he said about him as officer in charge of the case. As one small example he said about the still missing jewellry, 'It has either been disposed of by Hinds or may still be under his control.' Lord Goddard sentenced Hinds to twelve years.

Gridley (the night superintendent!), whom Sparks praised highly, got twelve *months*. It was incredible and due to the way Sparks spoke up for him, to his co-operation with the police. Nicholls and Martin, who had given evidence for Alfie, that he was not at Maples at all, got ten years each and Williams six years.

Alfie Hinds spent the next eleven years doing three things—escaping, protesting his innocence and litigating to that end. He brought proceedings and defended charges such as escaping in an unavailing effort to get his conviction reversed. He made two amazing escapes from prison—from Nottingham Prison and from Chelmsford Prison respectively, and spent his freedom, once two years, in the south of Ireland living in Ballsbridge, Monkstown and Greystones. He dealt in second-hand cars as a living.

He made one absolutely famous—hilarious—escape, when he locked his two escorting officers in a lavatory in the Law Courts in London, where he was litigating, and got clear away. But he was caught aboard an Aer Lingus plane at Bristol, just about to take off for Dublin. He loved Ireland, which was a strong point in his favour with me! He got nowhere with his protests on his litigation. Then after eleven years, Sparks published memoirs in the

Sunday Pictorial and described his greatest case, the Maples Robbery. He said—in terms—that Hinds did it, was the brains behind it, falsely denied having any part in it, and should take his punishment like a man.

Alfie Hinds sued him for libel. It was then possible in law to base a libel claim on the footing that one was wrongly convicted. After the Alfie Hinds civil case, that little known door was closed by what Bryan Anns and I called 'The Alfie Hinds Abolition Act', which made a conviction conclusive in libel.

The libel action was tried by Mr Justice Edmund Davies (later Lord Edmund-Davies) and a jury. It lasted twenty-six days. Contrast the one and a half days of the Old Bailey trial!

I led Bryan Anns for the plaintiff. We had a formidable team against us—Desmond Ackner QC and David Hirst (now Mr Justice Hirst). Outstandingly brilliant men; old friends and opponents of mine.

We had from early on a very hostile judge. A delightful man, but tough as they came and one who observed all the proprieties, but did not conceal his feelings.

Still Bryan Anns and I had an odd hunch that against this super-plus team—the judge (fresh from the Great Train Robbery trial), Dessie Ackner, David Hirst, and Sparks, we had—we might just have—the jury, the people who really mattered. We clung on like grim death to that hope.

When I was on my feet, hour after hour during those memorable four weeks, I had a 'feel'. We had the jury (I honestly think the judge and our opponents thought exactly the opposite). My hour to hour worry (Bryan's too): Could we hold them against that combination and in face of our obvious difficulties.

I heard later that a member of the jury fell in love with the lady juror who sat beside him, and she with him! They 'shared' documents; there were six copies of all documents, so two jurors had to 'share'. I also heard (we had 'grape-vines' too) that they got married. They were super. I'm sure they were very very happy.

I opened the case 'high'. Alfie was innocent—and Sparks knew it. The criminal trial was a disgrace. Please, jury, put it right. Find libel proved. As to damages, they were a subsidiary matter. Give him moderate damages, enough to register the injustice.

I called 'Peg'. With profound respect I feel that Mr Justice Edmund Davies (before him Lord Goddard) and Desmond Ackner 'played her' wrong. They painted her as a loyal 'wife' who was pitiable. They never faced up to the fact that she might be telling the truth.

I called Alfie Hinds—deliberately quite shortly in examination in chief. Bryan Anns, Percy Rolfe, and I had decided on that as the best tactics.

Desmond Ackner cross-examined him for five days—brilliantly, as one might expect. Dessie undoubtedly scored frequently. The judge plainly neither liked him nor believed him. We liked this! What we did not like was that Alfie lashed out at courts and lawyers indiscriminately.

We then called alibi witnesses, Martin, and expert witnesses as to the 'dust debris'. They completely discounted its incriminating value.

Desmond opened his case. The conviction was right. Alfie was a lying hypocrite. Cross-examining him was 'like cross-examining an electric eel'.

He called Sparks. I cross-examined him and concentrated strongly on the Old Bailey time and what he had said to the Lord Chief Justice about Hinds. He agreed that he had never met Hinds before the *Maples* case but held to all that he had said about him and went even further and said that he was the most dangerous criminal he had ever met in all his career. I led him on and suggested that he had no evidence of all this and was unfair to Hinds from the start. I got the feeling that the jury did not like this attitude by Sparks, and considered that the Old Bailey trial was unsatisfactory.

Tiddy and Budd were called as to the 'verbals'. The former was rude to me, which I welcomed, and surprisingly said that he did not know what 'verbals' were and had never heard the word before.

Gridley gave evidence and was a bad witness, hazy and hesitant. I cross-examined him, and I think it was effective as showing him to be unsatisfactory.

There was evidence about the 'dust debris' but we were now in a position to challenge it with our new evidence mentioned above.

Desmond Ackner and I addressed the jury. He stressed the 'wild allegations' which Alfie Hinds had made, and criticised his evidence strongly. He contrasted it with what he said was powerful of Sparks' case.

I asked the jury to regard the Old Bailey trial as a disgrace, to disbelieve Sparks, Gridley and the police officers who spoke as to the verbals, and to find for Hinds.

I knew that I had a hostile judge who would be speaking after me, and I stressed to the jury that they were the judges now. It was perhaps presumptuous of an Irishman but Chesterton had been quoted in the case and I ended by adapting a verse of his:

> Smile at us, pay us, pass us,
> But do not quite forget.
> We are the people of England
> And we haven't spoken yet.

The summing up of Mr Justice Edmund Davies conformed to the rules but was decidedly hostile to Alfie Hinds. No better indication of that was given than in his closing sentences where he contrasted the consequences of the case for respective parties and said that for Sparks to lose would mean 'red ruin' for him. Earlier he said, 'In the course of his opening, Mr Comyn, in ringing tones, said one of the most terrible things I have heard in the law. In the discharge of his duty he said, "This man Hinds is innocent, and Sparks knows it." If that be right, indeed it is one of the most dreadful things. I can remember myself no more shattering remark in over thirty years in the court than that.'

The jury were out for five hours and returned at 3.30 p.m. There was more than the usual tenseness as they slid in and took their places. Then the foreman announced that they found for the plaintiff Alfie Hinds and awarded him £1,300 damages. Costs followed.

Alfie was still in jail during the hearing, brought up from Parkhurst to Pentonville to be convenient to the Law Courts. With the announcement of the verdict the home secretary released him from prison immediately on parole.

After the case Alfie was determined to pursue yet another appeal to the Court of Criminal Appeal to get his conviction formally quashed, but I warned him strongly 'not to put his head in the lion's mouth again'. But he did and lost. I was ill at the time, but I would not have done the case in any event, because I felt strongly that he had achieved— against all the odds—all he could reasonably want.

Fortunately, the appeal to the Court of Criminal Appeal did not take away his freedom or take away anything from his remarkable success before the civil jury.

He subsequently led a very successful life. I periodically heard from him and he addressed me as 'Sir Jimmy', Jimmy being how I was universally known at the Bar. I was very sorry to hear of his death earlier this year.

John Murphy and Son Ltd

John Murphy was and is a remarkable man. He built up from nothing the construction and public works company which bears his name and does extensive business in English and Ireland. As contractors to a number of London boroughs and to a number of essential services there is hardly a hole in the road throughout London that has not got the Murphy sign 'buried' on it.

I emphasise that John Murphy personally was not involved in the case which I now mention, though he naturally took a lively interest in it and attended the Old Bailey regularly during the hearing, where I was defending.

The company, a subsidiary company and five executives were charged with conspiracy and fraud against the Revenue in paying workers full wages without tax on the pretext that they came from labour-supply companies, which were allegedly bogus, having been set up dishonestly for the purpose. This procedure was fairly common, because workmen do not like paying tax and welcome pay without deduction. It was known as The Lump, standing for lump sum payments.

The prosecution was in the hands of future high court judges John Leonard QC and Anthony Hidden. They had a heavy task wading through a mass of documents and seeking to tie up the accuseds' connection with the various companies.

In the end all were found Guilty. The two defendant companies between them were fined short of a million pounds, four of the accused got between five and two years imprisonment and one was put on probation.

John Murphy nicely asked me if there would be time to pay and we in fact got two years to do so.

Ginger

I went into court to judge how long the case before the one I was interested in was likely to last; I stayed because I got interested.

The man in the dock, charged with stealing a car, was in his later twenties and had a magnificent head of red hair. He was defending himself. The officer in charge of the case, who was obviously the last or second last witness for the prosecution, was in the witness-box giving evidence.

He was giving the most detailed evidence of arrest, evidently because the accused was alleged to have made oral confessions of guilt during the course of arrest.

Reading from his notebook the officer said, 'Having been admitted to the house by the landlady, Detective

Constable Brent and I proceeded to the third floor where we had ascertained that the accused had a single room. The door was locked from the inside and we accordingly knocked on it.' (He was of the old school, of course, who 'proceeded' and 'ascertained'.)

'A voice from inside said, "Who's that?"'

'I replied, "We are police officers and we wish to interview Mr John Smith. Are you he?"'

'He replied, "That's right, may I presume you've come about the car."'

'I said, "Would you open the door?"'

'He said, "Yes, certainly. Just let me get some clothes on".'

'I said, "Of course."' We waited a couple of minutes, and he opened the door. He asked us into the room and offered us a seat, which we took, and he sat on the end of his bed. I told him again what our enquiry was about and cautioned him. He then said, "I nicked the car alright. I got frightened soon after I done it and abandoned it in Kensington somewhere. Has it been found?" I said, "Yes, it had been found in Kensington as you say and considerably damaged."

He replied, "I didn't do no damage to it, at least I don't think I did. But as I tell you I was in a fair panic."

'I said, "Will you accompany us to the station?", and he answered, "I'll be glad to, can I make a written statement?" I told him he could, at the station, and I said, "Collect what you want to take with you". I gave him a cigarette and about five minutes later we departed for the station, where he was charged but did not in fact make any written statement.'

That was the end of the inspector's evidence and the judge asked the accused if he wanted to ask the officer any questions. Rising to his feet the prisoner said, 'I most certainly do.'

'You've given evidence of a lot of polite business about arresting me.'

'Yes.'

'It weren't like that at all.'

'It was exactly as I told my Lord and the jury.'

'My door weren't locked. You and the other bloke bashed it in.'

The inspector looked shocked and seemed devoid of speech.

'And I was in bed.'

'You were up when I saw you.'

'And your friend there threw himself on top of me'.

'Quite untrue.'

'While you said, "Got you, Ginger, you're for the high jump".'

'No.'

'You pulled me on to the bed and said, "Stick some clothes on and get cracking, Ginger, you're coming to the station if we have to drag you there".'

A look of outrage on his face and the officer shook his head.

'And I said, "What's this all about, mate?"'

'You didn't.'

'An' you said, "Wait and see, smart guy".'

'I did not.'

'You both got hold of me arms and pulled me downstairs to the car and the police station'.

I had to leave court then. About three quarters of an hour later, our case was called.

I had time to ask the clerk of the court whether there had been a verdict in the last case yet or were the jury still out. 'They were only about ten minutes', he said. 'Found him Not Guilty.'

Good old Ginger.

An Extraordinary 'Theft'

There should never have been a prosecution in the first place. But a prosecution having been launched, my junior

Michael Beloff, I think, my instructing solicitor (my old friend and client Frances Calderan of Theodore Goddard and Company) and I felt that it was going to be difficult to defend it successfully. And a finding of Guilty—any finding of Guilty (for there were alternative charges)— would be disastrous for our client, a senior director of a world-famous company. I am sorry to take refuge in anonymity but it would do no good at all to reveal names now and it would indeed do serious harm. The personal details are not necessary for the story I tell. So I will call him 'Mr A' and will similarly disguise other characters.

What happened was this. A rather tiresome London firm, consisting of two Indian gentlemen, brothers, regularly patronised the Nottingham factory of Mr A's group to repair certain fabrics for them.

Mr A's group dearly wished that 'Singh and Sons' would take their work elsewhere, because they were very very troublesome—constantly ringing up, constantly changing their minds about exactly what they wanted, impatient of delay, but themselves dilatory when asked for more precise instructions or about making payments. Still, there was no good reason for declining their work, telling them to take it (and it was considerable) elsewhere.

When Mr A was very busy, very hot and very bothered, one Summer afternoon, 'Mr Singh' senior insisted upon being got through to him on the telephone and, for the umpteenth time, wanted to know the progress of their latest order. He said they wanted it urgently, within seven days. Mr A was a kind, generous and courteous man, but these people tried his patience and that of his whole staff.

'I will make enquires', he said, 'and I'll ring you back.' His secretary made the necessary inquiries and found that on this occasion, by pure oversight, a serious oversight, the work had not even been started. It could be begun next morning but there was no hope whatsoever of the fabric (weighing about a ton) being back for at least a month.

Mr A was very perturbed. He did not relish having to ring Mr Singh senior. He delayed doing so and, of course, Mr Singh senior got through to him first.

'I was just about to ring you,' said Mr A.

'What is the news, will it be ready by tomorrow week?' enquired Mr Singh senior, in a good imitation of Peter Sellers. Mr A had been thinking about what to say, and so he replied politely, 'I have bad news for you. The consignment is missing and my staff really think it must have been stolen. I've very very sorry. We'll continue enquires and keep in touch with you.'

'My brother and I will be down in the morning and will expect to see you personally', said Mr Singh, ringing off. Poor Mr A panicked.

He got his secretary to ask the manager of the particular department concerned to come to see him immediately.

When the manager came to Mr A's office he was very worried that an oversight should have occurred, especially with regard to these people.

'Don't worry, Fred', said Mr A. 'I've had an idea, and I'll take full responsibility for it myself. Naturally there must be no sign of the stuff when the Singh Bros arrive here, at noon tomorrow.'

The manager nodded, in vigorous agreement.

'So', went on Mr A, 'get a lorry—I think Jimmy would be the best man—get the stuff loaded onto it and tell him to get "lost" for three or four days. He can, if necessary, pack it at my house, in the yard. Tell him in general terms what it's all about.'

Fred thought it an excellent idea and said he would get hold of Jimmy and have the idea put into execution right away. So he did, and then he and Mr A got on with their other work.

Next morning two angry 'Singh' brothers arrived with Mr A.

'A very bad business', said Mr Singh senior.

'Absolutely shocking', echoed Mr Singh junior.

'We'll sue you for thousands', both said, individually and together.

'We're insured and doubtless you are", Mr A pointed out after reluctant but inevitable grovelling apologies.

'Not the point', they said.

He could not understand why not.

'Very special order', they explained, 'very special customers.'

Then, taking him completely by surprise, Mr Singh senior said, 'You have of course informed police.'

Mr A had never thought of this.

'Well, not yet' he said.

'Must ring now, straight away', they said.

He had to. They sat there in his office until he did so.

He chose an inspector he knew (he would tell him, privately, after the Singhs had gone, the whole true story).

The Singhs stayed and stayed. They insisted upon being shown where the fabric had been kept before 'it went missing'. Mr A personally, and the manager personally, had to show them. Unfortunately the vacant space was deep in Warehouse 17A. And they plied Mr A and Fred with a series of searching questions. Was anything else missing? Why *their* fabric? Where could it have gone? Had there been any sign of a break-in? To take it away would have required a lorry—what was the security position at the points of exit? When was their consignment found to be missing? Etc.

Meantime there was a telephone call from the inspector for Mr A. An assistant secretary took the message down to Mr A where he, Fred and the angry Singh brothers were in Warehouse 17A.

The message was that an inspector and two officers would be over to see Mr A within an hour. Meantime, not to worry, enquires were in hand.

Mr A and Fred were very worried about this. They had to tell the Singhs, but with great presence of mind Mr A said that he insisted on seeing the officers on his own in the first place. (He would then tell them the precise position.)

Unfortunately, within the hour—before the inspector and officers could get down to the factory—the lorry and its contents had been located by the CID. It had been found, with Jimmy at the wheel, just emerging from Mr A's residence, heading west towards Manchester.

This dreadful news reached Mr A, again in the form of a secretary's message, just as he was about to take the Singhs from the warehouse to the local lunch room. He had felt that since they obviously had no intention of leaving before the police came, the least he could do was to give them lunch.

Well, the inspector and his officers came.

I suppose in a way, it had to be. But the charges could have been withdrawn later. Or could they?

Mr A (he alone) was charged with theft; later with alternatives, such as receiving stolen property.

Happily, he protested innocence and said nothing else. But got through to Mr Calderan. Naturally he got immediate bail.

Mr Calderan was through to me that evening.

The inspector was very distressed, and not a little puzzled. He has known Mr A for years, had frequently played golf with him; they had on occasion dined together with their wives and friends. A nicer more honest man, the inspector concluded, you could not meet.

On my advice we tried to get the summonses, which were to the Nottingham city magistrates, withdrawn. No good. To the reluctant police there seemed to be a strong case and of course the Singhs were sitting watching, watching like Indian hawks.

Should we go for trial? Or be tried summarily? And would the prosecution agree to the latter in view of the particular circumstances?

Michael Beloff, Mr Calderan and I were strongly in favour of summary trial. The unfortunate client was agreeable to take such course as we advised.

The prosecution were agreeable to summary trial. They briefed counsel.

I tried as hard as I could to get the case dropped. I met crown counsel at my chambers in London. I spoke to him in the robing room at Nottingham magistrates' court (a huge room in a huge building) on the morning fixed for the hearing.

I told him our case.

No good. All it did was to ease the inspector's mind. 'We can't, James; we're not unsympathetic, but put yourself in our shoes.' Most of my life had been spent putting myself in other people's shoes. They did not always fit. And of course I was by nature and practice a Defender. I had done reasonably few prosecutions.

Fortunately, there was minimum press representation, and the two representatives of 'the third estate' who were there (there were, I believe, five or seven courts actually sitting in that building that day) showed that they were thoroughly bored with this case. They hardly lifted a pencil throughout.

The Bench of three had an elderly man as chairman. Naturally I had found out as much about him as I could in the short time we had had his name. To his right was a man of similar age, who seemed to show in his face an ability for humour. The court was completed by a lady, married, about forty. She looked as if she had the art of 'understanding'.

Opposing counsel opened and conducted the case with complete fairness.

He called the two Singhs.

Before cross-examining I disclosed our case, in full. To give them their due the Singhs were understanding—angry, but understanding.

I had of course to call the client. I did at length. He swore (and, I was quite sure, truly) that he had no guilty mind (no *mens rea*) and had had no intention of depriving the owners of their property permanently.

He was cross-examined, quite shortly but skilfully. He readily agreed that what he had set in motion was absolutely stupid and that he should have realised it.

Michael Beloff called a character witness.

I addressed the Bench very briefly. I thought I sensed acceptance of my client's evidence, and sympathy.

They retired.

They asked for their clerk.

They were 'out' for a total of not more than fifteen minutes.

The chairman called up my client, who stood up, with military bearing.

'Mr A', he said, 'you acted in a very stupid way. We think you realise that now. We accept completely what you have told us. In the circumstances the summonses will be dismissed. We sincerely hope that this will not affect your distinguished career in any way.'

The client visibly showed his relief.

The chairman addressed himself to me: 'Mr Comyn, have you anything to say about costs?'

'Sir', I said, 'absolutely nothing. Absolutely nothing.'

'Very well.' And, as it turned out to be, there was not a word about the case in any papers and Mr A went on to further heights in the group.

12

Fleet Street and Bedford Square

The Crossman Diaries

RICHARD (DICK) CROSSMAN, who died in April 1974, was a public figure who achieved cabinet rank in the first Labour Government between 1964 and 1966. For many years Crossman had kept diaries, mostly via tapes, and he kept very detailed diaries when he became a member of the cabinet, a fact widely known to his cabinet colleagues and civil servants. He was a rebel and held strong views that there was too much secrecy about government. As far back as 1966 he entered into a contract with the *Sunday Times* to serialise his first volume covering his cabinet years 1964–66 preparatory to its publication as a book. Similar books were to follow for later years.

He appointed as his literary executors his wife, Michael Foot and Graham C. Greene of Jonathan Cape.

Over the years and particularly since the 1914–18 war innumerable books of political memoirs and recollections had been published, and though most of them had been officially vetted not all had been and there were anyway many 'indiscretions'. There had been quite an industry in this class of literature, and there still is.

In 1974 the secretary of the cabinet, Sir John Hunt, came to know about the first volume of the Crossman diaries and having seen it objected about it to the literary executors and the *Sunday Times*. He objected to breaches of cabinet secrecy, disclosure of discussions between ministers and with advisers, and details about the transfer and appointment of senior civil servants. Eventually getting on

for 150 specific 'breaches' were alleged under these heads
as well as 'grey areas' and the general tenor of the book.

The 'rules' contended for by Sir John Hunt and the
Government were translated under three heads called 'parameters' (I had never heard the word before). They were
based on the alleged 'doctrine' of collective responsibility
which precluded publishing (1) details of discussions in
cabinet or cabinet committee, any record of such discussions
and papers prepared for or arising out of these discussions;
(2) details of discussions or communications between
ministers and between ministers and advisers concerning
the development and formulation of policies and their
execution; (3) details of discussions and communications
between ministers and their advisers and the persons responsible for the appointment and transfer of senior members
of the public service and their fitness for positions of
responsibility.

No specific time limit was laid down. Nor was any
mentioned in the subsequent discussions apart from a very
general reference to the thirty-year limit of the Public
Records Act.

Richard Crossman recognised of course that there were
state secrets in the full sense. What he set himself against
were what he regarded as artificially created 'secrets' which
it was in the public interest to reveal, not conceal.

His first diary—a model for the others—was certainly
outspoken and undoubtedly contravened time and again
in letter and spirit each of the three parameters. But the
question was—were these specially composed 'parameters'
true rules, enforceable at law; were they truly as wide as
phrased and how long did they last?

The attorney general, Sam Silken, appeared for the
Crown. I led Charles Grey for the *Sunday Times* and Brian
Neill QC appeared for the literary executors.

The Crown had former lord chancellors, Lord Gardiner
and Lord Hailsham, Sir Peter (now Lord) Rawlinson
(former attorney general), Lord Diamond (former chief

secretary to the Treasury), Lord Butler (who had been home secretary, chancellor and deputy prime minister) and of course Sir John Hunt. All these witnesses stressed the tradition of 'confidentiality' in the process of inner government, the need for it if Government was to be properly conducted and the requirement of secrecy of discussion so that 'collective responsibility' should emerge. Some emphasised the privy councillors' oath. All implied a necessity for protection of advisers and civil servants.

For the *Sunday Times*, distinguished academics gave evidence, the effect of which was that there were no rules of law governing collective responsibility or confidentiality in respect of these matters. They were all matters for the taste and good sense of the person concerned. They delved far back into history, politics and the law. These witnesses were Godfrey Le May (a fellow and tutor in politics in Oxford); John P. Mackintosh (author of *The British Cabinet* and a former professor of politics); Professor Wade (professor of English law at Oxford), who said powerfully that a 'convention' was by its description and nature not enforceable at law; and Dr Middlemas (lecturer in modern history). We then had the journalists' views from Harold Evans (editor of the *Sunday Times*); William Rees-Mogg (editor of *The Times*, now Lord Rees-Mogg), and Peter Jenkins (of the *Guardian*). Finally we had the political and general witnesses—Lord Houghton (ex-cabinet minister), who knew about Crossman diarying for publication and said it was generally known and in no way inhibiting to colleagues; Jo Grimond MP of the Liberal party; Jeremy Bray MP, two TV witnesses about making a film inside Whitehall committees, and Sir Anthony Nutting (former minister of state at the foreign office).

Two of those witnesses need elaboration—Dr Middlemas and Sir Anthony Nutting.

Dr Middlemas listed a number of authors whom he said had breached the alleged 'parameters'—Sir John French, Lord Beaverbrook, Admiral Jellicoe, Lloyd George, Sir

Henry Wilson, Lord Grey, Lord Haldane, Asquith, Winston Churchill, Hugh Dalton, Francis Williams, Lord Birkenhead, Michael Foot, George Brown, etc. etc.

We also alleged breaches of the 'parameters' by Harold Wilson himself in his book *The Labour Government of 1964–70*. Sir John Hunt acknowledged two, but as being reasoned exceptions to the accepted general rule.

Sir Anthony Nutting told how he resigned over the Suez War but after a purposeful ten-year delay decided to give his account. In spite of cabinet secretarial opposition, but making some concessions to it, he published his book *No End of a Lesson*.

Brian Neill read the evidence of the three literary executors—Janet Morgan (Crossman's historical assistant), who said that national security apart he had said to her that the only constraints he recognised upon his freedom to publish were academic integrity and good taste; Lord Gordon-Walker (former cabinet minister), as to a book of his own which in places exceeded the 'parameters'; Lord Kennett (parliamentary secretary at Crossman's ministry part of the time), who said it was common knowledge that not only Crossman but other ministers were keeping diaries for publication; Rudolph Klein, as to Hugh Dalton's diaries; and John Montgomerie (solicitor) as to his efforts to edit volume I of the diaries to meet the requirements of the cabinet office—a truly gargantuan task!

Then came additional evidence from Lord Gordon-Walker and Houghton that they did not know of the 'parameters' when they were in office. I cross-examined Sir John Hunt, a most delightful man but a strong minded senior 'public servant'.

After the evidence followed the arguments. They were broadly on the Crown's side a tradition and need for secrecy about the deliberations and decisions of inner government; on our two sides the absence of any clear rules and the unenforceability of the 'parameters' by legal action. Brian Neill stressed that if there were to be sanctions they were disciplinary, not legal and, most important, that this particular diary related to eleven years ago. He joined with me in submitting that alleged public interest did not give a cause for action and that 'confidentiality' did not give the attorney general grounds for claim. He posed the question forcefully as to how long the protection was supposed to last. And he said that to succeed the attorney general had to prove in respect of each passage complained of a breach of some substantive right.

The attorney general pressed his right to act 'in the public interest', prayed in aid the inherent obligations of cabinet ministers and privy councillors; he stressed 'collective responsibility', pointed to the mischiefs of disclosure and relied strongly on 'confidentiality'.

The lord chief justice reserved his judgment over the long vacation. Charles Grey and I, and I think all of us on the defence side were pessimistic.

When the judgment came, on the first day of the new legal year in October, it did not attempt to go into every nook and cranny of the argument. It rejected out of hand what we had regarded as the dangerous claim that public interest alone—or rather alleged public interest—gave the attorney general a cause of action without more. It accepted, however, the doctrine of 'collective responsibility', the basics of cabinet secrecy and the right of the attorney general to sue for breach of confidentiality. The claims in respect of civil servants were rejected. The attorney general's main arguments thus succeeded, but Lord Widgery said that there must be a limit and that having read the book and considered the evidence he thought that after eleven years there was no longer any need for protection and he would not restrain publication. So the attorney general lost the case. There was no appeal and the diary and its successors went ahead.

I personally was very well satisfied but I gather that many people were not completely satisfied. That is usually the hallmark of a good judgment!

13

R. v. Cairns, Aitken, Roberts *and the* Sunday Telegraph

A CONTROVERSIAL PROSECUTION at the Old Bailey arose out of the Nigerian Civil War of 1967–70, when the state of Biafra fought for independence from the Federated Military Government of Nigeria.

There was much sympathy for Biafra in England and Ireland and throughout the world. Much criticism too of the supplying of arms by Britain and other countries to the Government of Nigeria. Doubt also among pro-Biafrans as to the true extent of British supplies to the central Government.

There was a British High Commission to the central Government and by 1969 the defence adviser to it had been for some time Colonel Robert E. Scott. There was also an international team of military observers concerned with all humanitarian aspects of the war on both sides. For a short time the senior British representative on it had been a very distinguished soldier, Major-General Henry Templar Alexander. By 1969 he had been replaced in that position first by another and then by Colonel Douglas (Duggie) Cairns, a former army colleague and close friend of his, actively suggested by him for the appointment.

In 1969 Jonathan Aitken, a young free-lance journalist in his late twenties and a prospective Conservative parliamentary candidate, went to Nigeria and Biafra and on the introduction of Major-General Alexander had informal, non-attributable, conversations with among others Colonel Scott and Colonel Cairns. He was disgusted with what he saw, was convinced of large British supplies to the Federal Government and was strongly in sympathy with Biafra which was holding out—as he thought it would indefinitely— with 30,000 troops against 120,000. He wrote articles (entirely unobjectionable) and made his views widely known.

Major-General Alexander, a friend and constituent of Jonathan Aitken, did not share his views and in an effort to enlighten him gave him after a dinner party on 21 December 1969 a copy of a very detailed Report by Colonel Scott running to ninety-one paragraphs, and entitled 'An Appreciation of the Nigerian Conflict', with the word 'Confidential' typed on the outside. The general maintained that he stressed the confidentality to Aitken.

Some fifty-one copies of this report had been circulated and one had gone to Colonel Cairns, who had sent a copy to his old friend and predecessor, Major-General Alexander.

The report covered all aspects of the war, including British supplies, and in certain respects was critical of the Nigerian Government and forces.

Jonathan Aitken ran off some copies and gave two to his pro-Biafra colleague, the Rt Hon. Hugh Fraser MP, to use generally and for the purpose of asking questions in the House.

Believing the report to be important for the information of the British public, Jonathan Aitken after Christmas arranged for its issue through literary agents (directing the fee to go to Biafran charity). The sale was to the *Sunday Telegraph*, whose editor was Brian Roberts.

The *Sunday Telegraph* claimed to have got complete Government clearance for it through the usual Government channels, but on the other side it was said that clearance was given concerning national security but a warning given about the Official Secrets Acts and the general undesirability of publication.

At any rate the *Sunday Telegraph* published the report on 11 January 1970 and other newspapers took it up. Ironically almost contemporarously news was coming in about the imminent collapse of Biafra. This proved to be true and was appreciably earlier than informed forecasts.

Publication of the report enraged the Nigerian Government and Colonel Scott had to leave shortly afterwards. It also angered and embarrassed the British Government, causing diplomatic strain between it and Nigeria.

To the general surprise a prosecution was launched. This was under section 2 of the Official Secrets Acts 1911 for possessing and receiving and also for communicating—as the case might be—unlawful information. The accused were Colonel Cairns (for whom I appeared), Jonathan Aitken (represented by Basil Wigoder QC, now Lord Wigoder), and the *Sunday Telegraph Ltd* and its editor Brian Roberts (Jeremy Hutchinson QC, now Lord Hutchinson). Others who received or passed on the report were not prosecuted. Hugh Fraser MP specifically invited prosecution, Major-General Alexander was not prosecuted but was a crown witness.

Preliminary proceedings at the Guildhall Magistrates' Court lasted many days because the main Crown witnesses, Colonel Scott and Major-General Alexander, were cross-examined at length. The Crown was represented by John Mathew (of the Father Mathew family), treasury Counsel. In opening the case he was lenient and understanding in respect of my client, Colonel Cairns, but not so in the case of the others. He said the case was of great national importance.

Which makes it more odd that at one stage there were out of court discussions between all parties about the matter being disposed of before the magistrates rather than being sent on to the Old Bailey. This would be on the basis of pleas of guilty and small fines, with suitable statements on all sides—a general playing down of everything. My client, on, and independent of, my advice, would not have it. He had a good character and record (as did the others). We were not prepared to compromise his record or to jeopardise the critical position he now occupied with one of the big banks. Accordingly the matter proceeded.

The magistrates duly committed all defendants for trial, and with a general election announced the unfortunate Jonathan Aitken next day had to resign as Conservative parliamentary candidate for his constituency (Thirsk and Malton).

On 12 January 1971 (just a year after the newspaper publication) a three and a half week trial opened at the Old Bailey before Mr Justice Caulfield and a jury.

The Crown case was that the Scott Report contained confidential information, unauthorised disclosure of which would be contrary to the interests of the State. It was 'an official secret' stamped 'Confidential'. Colonel Cairns had received it in confidence and had no right to pass it on to Major-General Alexander. The latter had given it to Jonathan Aitken on a confidential, non-attributable basis. Aitken had abused the confidence. The *Sunday Telegraph* and its editor knew—had been warned—that publishing it would contravene the Act.

My case for Colonel Cairns was that he was an independent mission of his own, entitled to receive and pass on any document he thought fit: also that the Scott Report was not secret or confidential in any way and stamping on a document 'Confidential' or 'Secret' did not make it so.

The other defendants took the secrecy point very strongly and stressed that they came by the report innocently.

The Crown's case and witnesses were as in the magistrates' court. The judge quickly showed a very favourable view of Colonel Cairns.

One moment of humour occurred when I was cross-examining Mr. Welser of the Foreign Office:

Q. Would it be right to say that nowhere can we find any written rules about classifications?

A. Quite wrong.

Q. Then there are, are there, written notes about classification?

A. Yes, but they are probably themselves classified.

This was matched by the defence witness, Major Gray, who worked with Colonel Scott in the final stapling of the report. He said, 'I remember Colonel Scott saying that the he had marked his Report confidential in order to ensure a wide distribution'.

At the end of the crown case we all submitted No Case to Answer. I was hopeful for my client, whom everybody regarded with sympathy and the judge with favour. But the submissions were all summarily rejected. Perhaps, as sometimes happens, the judge wanted to get the jury's verdict on the matter.

I called Colonel Cairns, a man of near sixty, of distinguished record and distinguished appearance. He told of receiving a copy of the report from Colonel Scott and of seeing nothing wrong in sending a copy to his friend, Major-General Alexander.

When Colonel Cairns was being cross-examined by John Mathew the judge intervened and said, 'Throw your shoulders back, Colonel, and tell the jury who you were.'

The colonel replied, 'I was the senior British member of the International Observer Team.'

The judge went on, 'And you thought you were doing your duty in sending the report?'

'Yes, my Lord.'

The interventions were helpful!

We called next Brigadier Sir Bernard Fergusson, former governor-general of New Zealand, successor of Major-General Alexander as head of the Observer Team and with Colonel Cairns then his deputy. He paid high tribute to Colonel Cairns. He said that he might well have forwarded the report as Colonel Cairns had done and that in the circumstances it seemed to him 'morally all right'.

John Aitken and Brian Roberts were in their turn impressive witnesses. John Aitken had naturally to face a severe attack as to the terms on which he got the report from Major-General Alexander. There were strict conditions, which he had broken, said the Crown. There were not, he said; Major-General Alexander's evidence was wrong.

John Aitken called guests from the Alexander dinner party and Mr Hugh Fraser MP. Also strong character witnesses in Charles Wintour, editor of the *Evening Standard*, and the then speaker of the house of commons, the Rt Hon. Selwyn Lloyd. The effect of the character evidence was that John Aitken was a reliable and trustworthy journalist and person.

It was clearly at John Aitken that the Crown were aiming their main guns. The Crown were relying strongly on Major-General Alexander's account of attaching conditions to the report and Aitken frequently breaking those conditions—and now lying about the matter.

The case for Brian Roberts and the *Sunday Telegraph* was that they had acted innocently and in good faith and that there was nothing secret about the report.

Mr Roberts described a free press as he saw it and the duty to inform the public unless direct national interest under the Official Secrets Act was under threat. He also commented on the meaninglessness of 'Confidential' in respect of this story.

His colleague, assistant editor Gordon Smith-Shepherd, said that in his contact with the foreign office about the matter there was no prohibition, in reference to the Official Secrets Act—simply a hope that the report would not be published.

After the evidence came final speeches. The unfortunate jury had by then heard eight speeches from counsel; four opening and four closing, including of course the prosecution.

Mr Justice Caulfield summed-up for a day and a half. It was a meticulous summing-up and left all relevant points to the jury. There was a strong indication that they might decide to acquit Colonel Cairns and as the summing-up developed a lesser indication that they might decide to acquit the others as well. There was a strong condemnation of section 2 of the Official Secrets Act, and heavy stress on the freedom of the press. He ruled that as a matter of law anybody handling a document from an official source which was marked 'Confidential' was not necessarily breaking the law.

It was terrible to think of Colonel Cairns, and the others, having to go to the court cells every day during intervals. At night they were on bail.

The jury were out for just over two hours. They then brought in a verdict of Not Guilty against all defendants.

Well, none of us anticipated getting our costs—but we did.

Thus ended a case presented as a Rocket, which turned out to be a Damp Squib.

14

Religious Affairs

I HAVE HAD QUITE A NUMBER of 'religious' cases, cul-
minating of course in the 100-day Moonies case which I
tried as a judge.

In a divorce case called *Pais v. Pais* against my old
friend Roger Gray from chambers, I tried to establish for
the Catholic Church privilege for a priest as to the confes-
sional and confidential conversations. I failed—as I believe
I would in Ireland—but my priest was given privilege, in
common with laymen, in respect of marriage counselling
and attempts at reconciliation of spouses; a privilege which
was that of the party and not of the priest, so that the
party could waive it, as this one did. This must be accepted
as the best word on priests' privilege in England, but it is
right to point out that I have found the English courts,
civil and criminal, always anxious to avoid confrontation
with a priest on this subject.

Christian Science I have met more than once. In one
case I was instructed by the Official Solicitor (official guardian of minors) to apply to the court for an order that a
seriously ill child should have an operation, contrary to the
wishes of his Christian Science parents. The court duly made
the order.

Shortly before I became a judge I had a most interesting
criminal appeal, *R. v. Baeur*. The accused stabbed a girl
and it was agreed that if she had accepted a blood transfusion she would have lived. But knowing that otherwise
she would die she refused on religious grounds to have the
blood transfusion, and she died. The accused was charged
with murder and convicted. We appealed and argued that

death was not caused by him but by her. The court took
the line that death was due to his act of stabbing. We
replied that a new act, refusal of the blood transfusion,
had intervened. A lot of old cases were referred to. The
court accepted the Crown's argument and dismissed the
appeal. I was disappointed because I thought there was a
lot in our argument and one could not have stronger facts.

On one occasion I acted for a man, whom I will call G,
who was under a mental disability and hence was represented by the Official Solicitor. He was defending a petition
for divorce by his wife on the ground of cruelty. He was a
tragic figure, and one of the saddest features of the case
was that he encountered his brother in a mental hospital
in Dublin.

His strange beliefs included one that he would not allow
anyone to act for him who showed a red light, as distinct
from a blue light, over his head when he swung his watch
over the head. He asked the Official Solicitor and me to
undergo the test, and we agreed. The light was apparently
blue in both cases, so we were able to act.

The cruelty case was not very strong, but the wife was,
principally because of a curious allegation which infuriated
the judge. Mr G admitted that after his wife and children
left him he addressed a series of postcards to her at her
father's, Lord X's, country house in her maiden name.
She—and the judge—regarded this as insulting and humiliating. But according to his view of things Mr G had an
explanation; she had left him and therefore reverted to her
single status.

Speaking of the Official Solicitor acting for people under
mental instability, he once briefed me to apply to the
court about a 'dispute' between two patients regarding a
sum of over £300,000 won in the football pools. It was
the absolute reverse of the kind of dispute one would find
in the outside world, because here each patient was insisting
that the other was entitled to the lot! They had put up the

stakes equally, one had picked the teams, the other had made the entry in his sole name. The latter said that the one who had picked the teams was entitled to the money, but he said that his friend having signed the entry should get the money. The court did not need much persuading to order half to each, to be held in trust.

For about three years I acted for the Church of Scientology, founded by Ron Hubbard, and having its English headquarters at East Grinstead in Sussex, where it runs courses for the numerous people interested. It is a religious, scientific, philosophical organisation and has an extensive special vocabulary of its own. During my association with it, it had a good deal of litigation and other legal work conducted by a special and very efficient legal department of its own.

I am afraid I did not not have much success for the Scientologists. No doubt that is why they left me, but the amusing thing is that they went instead to a counsel who had appeared against us and who had poured ridicule on Scientology, the Scientologists and Mr Ron Hubbard, positively laughing at the words and phrases used by the group. The counsel was none other than Quintin Hogg, later lord chancellor. The clients obviously recognised his unique talents, so long known to all of us, and felt it better to have him for them than against them. In my days with them one master actually said to me, 'I never find for the Scientologists.'

I was once instructed for a case in the Court of Appeal by a religious organisation notoriously adverse to the Catholic Church. At the eve of hearing conference I pointed out to them that I was a Catholic and did they really want me to do their case. They said yes: the reason they had come to me was because I was a Catholic and they wanted to show the court that they had no religious prejudices! They lost!

Quite the most bizarre religious case I had concerned a
man from the Medway Towns and was, of all things, a
planning application.

He had founded a religion and had one adherent, a very
wealthy widow. She died and left him two million pounds
on condition that he built a church in the Medway Towns.
After some difficulty he found a site but, opposed by
pretty well everybody who could oppose, he was refused
planning permission. This was the appeal, to an inspector.

At the conference before the hearing I ventured to
point out that a difficulty we faced was that there was only
one member of the Church—himself.

'You're Catholic?', he said. I said, 'Yes'.

'Well, your religion started with one person', he said.

I was a bit flummoxed by that observation but eventually
said, 'Wouldn't a small church building do for a while?'
He liked the idea; it would save money. And he readily
agreed to let me alter the size at the enquiry; in fact to
amend or alter *anything* to get planning permission.

We faced an irascible and impatient inspector at the
enquiry. At one stage he appeared to be suggesting that
my client had conned the old lady out of two million
pounds, but I pointed out that she had not just left him
the money but had made a condition about the building
of a church.

He then turned his attention, sarcastically, to what he
called 'this one-man church', whereupon I unashamedly
borrowed my client's answer to me the night before. It
did not go down well.

I tried everything. That there was freedom of religion
in England, that nobody should be prejudiced for his
religion, that the land would have to be filled with something, so why not a church, and that the objections were
ridiculous—for example, the ones that claimed there
would be increased traffic.

It was all no good. The inspector said that he would
report in due course. We knew how he would—and he did.

The client was grateful but sad. I'm afraid I never knew if he got the two million pounds. Before we parted I suggested that he might build a small addition to his house and have the church there.

When I was a judge I had to decide in one case whether there had been blasphemy of Mahomet. I held that there could only be blasphemy of Jesus Christ. I was glad to see that there was a similar decision recently.

15

Miss B and April Ashley

Miss B

MISS B WAS A PROSTITUTE in Blackpool. Except in prostitution she had no record. Then suddenly she was convicted and charged with luring a man on to the sands for two colleagues of hers—so it was alleged—to rob him, which they did.

She received an impeccable trial (that was the trouble), was found Guilty and sentenced to four years imprisonment.

I was briefed in the appeal to the Court of Criminal Appeal. They, like me, felt that there was something disquieting about the case, but they felt obvious difficulty about interfering when there had been a full and fair trial.

Counsel for the Crown then intervened to say that it had just been discovered that one of the witnesses against Miss B, an alleged eyewitness, had a previous conviction for stealing, which the defence had of course not known about.

This made all the difference. Perhaps stretching things a bit the CCA said that if this had been known to the jury at trial it might 'well have affected their verdict'.

So Miss B was set free.

My instructing solicitor and I met her at the door to the cells. She was a pathetic figure, in tears and wearing (it was now November) only the light dress which she had on when she was arrested in June. We took her for coffee and found that she had been supplied only with a single ticket to Blackpool—the scene of all her trouble—and a couple of pounds.

We both tried to persuade her to stay in London and give up prostitution. We would help her to get accommodation and a job. But she strongly resisted our offers, saying that Blackpool was the only place she knew and prostitution the only occupation. We had to accept this but told here that we would inform the welfare people in Blackpool and ask them to help on arrival.

My instructing solicitor took her off to buy a coat for her. We heard no more of Miss B until a few years ago to my horror I saw a photograph of her on the front page of the *Daily Express*—as one of the latest victims of a series of murders of prostitutes on the tow-path of the Thames.

Poor Miss B. She was a nice girl.

April Ashley—Sex Change

April Ashley was reluctantly brought up as male, reluctantly because her physical and mental feelings and inclinations were entirely feminine. At the age of twenty-six she went through an operation in Casablanca which removed her physical signs of manhood and provided her to the point of perfection with the sexual organs of a woman. All that was missing was the ability to conceive. Full details of the operation have not been forthcoming as the surgeon from Casablanca has not been willing to come forward.

After the operation, April Ashley also bore all the physical appearances of a woman and was treated by the state authorities in England, such as the National Health, as a woman. She lived the life of a woman and was so universally recognised.

After the operation a man named Arthur Corbett, with full knowledge of her history, became infatuated with her in his own words ' as a man for a woman'. He left his wife and children for her and pursued her seeking to persuade her to marry him. She was reluctant to marry but eventually agreed and they went through a ceremony of marriage in Gibraltar.

148 *Summing It Up*

They did not live together for long and Corbett then petitioned the English court for nullity on the grounds (1) that April Ashley was a man, and a man cannot marry a man and (2) that the marriage, if there were one, had not been consummated by reason of the respondent's incapacity or alternatively wilful refusal.

Representing April Ashley Leonard Lewis and I contended (a) that she was a woman, (b) that the petitioner was estopped by his conduct from asserting otherwise or obtaining a decree of nullity against her, and (c) that if there was to be nullity it should be in favour of the respondent (a person being able to get a decree on her own incapacity).

The trial came before Mr Justice Ormrod, formerly of our chambers, later a Lord Justice. He was a doctor.

The parties gave evidence and so did three distinguished specialists on each side.

The judge did not seem very impressed by my points against the petitioner's conduct which I regarded as quite shocking. He deserted his family for my client and having all the facts he persuaded her into marrying him. I could not think of stronger merits on her side, yet the judge early seemed to show favourableness to Mr Corbett and his case.

The doctors gave interesting evidence, three as to why April Ashey should be regarded as a male, three as to why she should be treated as a woman.

There were chromosome tests and they were predominantly male.

Our main argument was that if April Ashley were not a woman before the operation she had marked feminine characteristics and by the operation became a woman and was also treated generally and by the law. Why not for the purpose of marriage, all material facts being known by both parties? After all, the law did not in the ordinary way require a person to disclose his or her impotence or physical abnormality or lack of virginity—and these marriages were valid.

The judge found against April Ashley on every point. He held that she was and always had been a male, that the so-called marriage was a nullity, that the decree should go to Mr Corbett, that estoppel did not apply in law and that he had no discretion to refuse the relief claimed by Mr Corbett. Sex, he said, was determined at birth and a so-called 'sex-change' operation could not change already determined sex.

I thought the overall decision was hard upon April Ashley and feel that at very least the justice of the case required a decree for her and not for Corbett.

There was no appeal but at least she walked out of court to a world which recognised and treated her as a woman—a very likeable woman.

The Book

I was briefed to defend S at the Old Bailey for offences against boys—for which he had previous convictions. He instructed me to put certain questions to the boys which I refused to do and, for one of the rare occasions at the Bar, I declined to act for him. He decided to appear for himself.

Since this happened shortly before trial I thought it right in the client's interests to attend the opening of the trial and explain, tactfully, to the trial judge, that I would not be appearing and the client would act in person. Judge Alan King Hamilton did not relish the prospect of the accused acting for himself in a case of this nature and tried to make me carry on, but, without giving anything away, I was adamant that I would not be acting.

About two weeks later I got a message from the court that S had been convicted and the judge would appreciate it if I could attend and make a plea in mitigation.

This was all very surprising and unusual; indeed unique in my experience. After all, the judge had heard the case, which I had not, and he had in the form of antecedents all the history of the prisoner before him. Naturally in the interests of the client I complied, having first got from the client some some further details about himself and about how the trial had developed.

I then made my plea in mitigation, but in the light of his previous offences S was sentenced to ten years.

I saw him a couple of occasions afterwards at Reading Gaol (shades of Oscar Wilde). The first was about a possible appeal to the Court of Criminal Appeal, which I advised against. The second was to advise him about the form of a petition to the European Court which he was determined to make. Advising him against it as being hopeless, I nevertheless helped him as far as I could with the necessary documentation.

On the second occasion he told me that he had written a book of which he produced the manuscript entitled 'The Alleged Crime of Sodomy'. He said he would like to dedicate it to me. I was shaken by the suggestion and sought in every way I could to put him off. If the book ever got published the dedication would naturally be most embarrassing to me—especially as I expected that the contents would be as explosive as the title. He alarmed me by claiming that he had a publisher. Eventually I managed to dissuade him by inventing a rule at the Bar that prevented books being dedicated to us.

His case was sad as so many such cases are. He had an excellent family background, he was talented and clever, he had had good employment, he enjoyed a good standard of living. All that was wrong—and of course it was a lot—was his predilection for boys, in which he saw nothing wrong at all. As my interview at Reading Gaol showed, conviction and that further period of imprisonment had done nothing at all to change his views. To him 'unnatural offences' were profoundly natural.

I have, thankfully, not heard of the book.

One other client I declined to act for was a well-known MP's wife who wanted to include in her cruelty divorce an allegation that he was a transvestite who roamed the streets at night dressed as a woman. I told her that she had enough without that—and that it would ruin her husband and seriously affect their two teenage boys. She insisted and I told her she'd better go elsewhere. She did; the allegation was included and the husband *was* ruined.

16

Family Affairs

A Missing Wife

THERE IS A POPULAR misconception that you cannot have a murder charge without a body. This is quite wrong. In 1884—in Exeter—a man called Dudley and a man called Stephens were tried for the murder of a young seamate of theirs, when they were lost at sea, in bad weather. It was a very gruesome case. Driven desperate, and at the point of starvation, they had killed him—and eaten him. About the absence of a body, it was admitted that they had killed a man, and there was no body because they had eaten him. The point raised in their defence was—Necessity. It was held to be an unavailing defence; they were found guilty of murder and sentenced to death. They were reprieved. It is not, I think, generally realised that they were in fact released after six months. I simply cannot think why.

Then in 1951—again on the Western Circuit, this time at Winchester, a ship's steward named Camb was tried for the murder of a pretty girl passenger, 'Gay' Gibson, whom he admitted pushing out of the porthole when the ship was at sea. No body. No matter. He accepted that he had pushed her out of the porthole into the sea and that she had been lost at sea. He was running the line that he had some sort of defence—provocation, sexual, frenzy, whatever.

Mr Justice Hilbery, that tall, stern, unsmiling, formidable judge, was not having any of that.

Camb was convicted and sentenced to death. He was lucky not to be hanged. It was at a time when the death penalty was, to quote the common phrase which I also found chilling, 'in suspense'.

Another thing that is not generally known: released on parole after serving a long term of imprisonment Camb changed his name and went to Scotland; where—under that name—he was later again charged with murder; and again convicted.

In 1974 I was instructed to lead David Owen Thomas QC and Graham Neville in defence of an army captain, Captain Symonds, on a charge that he had murdered his wife ten years before. There was no body (we made a lot of play of that point), but she had not been seen or heard of for ten years. The prosecution team was as nice, as fair as one could wish for, but as thorough and as formidable as one could fear—T. Hampden Inship QC leading Martin Tucker.

The trial judge was Peter Bristow, Mr Justice Bristow—always a welcome tribunal, because he was a fair and just man, as well as being a delightful one.

For the defence we had our difficulties. Oh yes, we had our difficulties. Captain and Mrs Symonds had lived near the sea and near Dartmoor. Mrs Symonds had 'disappeared', albeit ten years before, 'abandoning' a much loved little boy of four. Within days our client had installed his mistress in his (his wife's, his baby son's) house—as 'wife and mother'. When the police took the matter of his disappeared wife up with him he had lied, changing his 'story' more than once. He had eventually said, and this was the case we were instructed to put forward, that one morning ten years ago he had dropped his wife at a supermarket—and had never seen or heard of her again.

We had the good fortune to be instructed by an absolutely superb young local solicitor named Brabin, a relation of that wholly delightful judge, 'Danny' Brabin. Young Mr Brabin had obtained for us, after a great deal of hard work, a mass—a veritable mass—of important information. It included detailed statistics of the astonishing large number of people who 'disappear completely' every year in Britain, the variety of reasons apart from being murdered as to why they disappear, full details of all tides and winds around the date of the alleged murder, particulars of all weapons and ammunition which Captain Symonds could have obtained, information as to where a body would have been washed up at that time if dumped at sea at various points along the south coast of England, and a complete 'geography' of Dartmoor, including its caves, pits, crevices etc.

We had three or four consultations in prison with Captain Symonds, a middle-aged, cheery man, who had a splendid handle-bar moustache. We had been round Dartmoor, looking into caves, and pits, scraping around and finding old bones (of sheep and goats).

David Owen Thomas, my wife Anne and I were staying for the trial at local, delightful, Moretonhampstead, in the Railway Hotel at the edge of Dartmoor, which I had first come to know (but not to afford) as a young Western Circuiteer. It has a picturesque, tricky, little golf course beside it, in its grounds. (A Dartmoor stream runs through the golf course and I spent one evening during the case with David Owen Thomas splashing in and out of the stream after errant balls.) My ever-loving, ever-helpful, wife did not on this occasion help things, or boost my morale, by looking out of our bedroom window the first morning at Dartmoor and saying, 'So that is where Mrs Symonds presumably is.'

I have, I think, something of 'a jury instinct'. (My father told me once of a jury advocate on the old Munster Circuit who woke up one morning during Cork Assizes to find his left eye swollen up and nearly closed. In the robing room before court he was in a dreadful state, moaning 'My jury eye, my jury eye. I can't open my jury eye'.)

I was pretty apprehensive about the people being sworn in to try Captain Symonds. So were David Owen Thomas and Graham Neville. The eventual twelve jurors were a bunch of tough-looking, unsympathetic, Devonians, who seemed to me as if they loved their wives and dogs. All were men. We probably had had this much luck; there wasn't a woman on the jury.

When called upon to plead, Captain Symonds, smartly dressed in country clothes and sporting that magnificent moustache and a cheery look, beamed at Mr Justice Bristow and in a good, loud, military voice said, 'I am NOT GUILTY, my Lord.' If we of the defence team had anything to do with it, these were the only words we were going to let him speak during the whole proceedings.

Hampden Inship of course opened the Crown case beautifully. He had his difficulties, too—murder as far back as ten years ago; ludicrously 'open' behaviour by Captain Symonds. But he drove home, drove well home, the Crown's strong points: the last person known to have been with her was her husband, Captain Symonds; most mysterious, complete disappearance; the unbelievable abandonment of a much loved little boy; when Captain Symonds was later asked about it all he lied; why did he lie?; and he showed no kind of sadness at all; he had installed his mistress in the house within a few days; if his wife had suddenly vanished from a supermarket, as he now said, why had he done nothing at all about it—not reported it to the police for example? Circumstantial evidence; circumstantial, yes, but very strong. Burden of proof on the Crown, but they would submit in due course proved beyond all reasonable doubt as murder, murder by Captain Symonds.

The Crown called their witnesses, to prove these matters. I was in fact able to make quite a lot of headway with them in cross-examination. First, the enormous delay in anybody doing anything about it. If Captain Symonds' inactivity was surprising was not that of his wife's relations, their friends, their neighbours, the police, quite incredible? And then I was able to bring out all the mass of material which Mr Brabin had provided us with. How exactly was it suggested Captain Symonds had murdered her? In what manner? Where? We (via Mr Brabin) had explored every possible avenue: had they, the Crown, done so? It pretty soon became apparent that, excellent though the prosecution research had been, that of Mr Brabin had been even better. He had asked all the right questions and had details in depth to answer them.

I had kept a good eye on the jury all through. They did not like my client. They did not like me. They would interpret silence on his part as guilt.

The Crown closed their case on the morning of the fifth day, the Friday.

I got up to face Mr Justice Bristow—and old friend, an old colleague, and old fellow Circuiteer. An outstanding judge. A grand lawyer. A shrewd, down-to-earth, man. Patient, courteous, only rarely intervening. Always with a kind, disarming (sometimes deceptive) smile.

Casting a hostile eye on the hostile jury, I said, with some satisfaction, 'My Lord, on behalf of the defence, we call no evidence.'

Mr Justice Bristow bowed.

'And I have a submission to make, my Lord. A submission of No Case to Answer.' With increased satisfaction I looked at the jury, 'I will be inviting your Lordship to withdraw this case from the jury or to *direct* them to bring in a *verdict of Not Guilty.*'

They could have hit me.

I developed our submissions. Suspicion—but suspicion is not proof. The Crown had a heavy burden of proof. They had to make the jury *sure* in order to obtain a conviction. *Sure*—beyond all reasonable doubt.

There was, we submitted, insufficient material here to meet that test. If a conviction ensued the Court of Criminal Appeal would have to quash it as being 'unsafe and unsatisfactory'.

I spoke for about three quarters of an hour. Hampden Inship for perhaps a little longer.

Mr Justice Bristow did not retire. He said that suspicion, even grave suspicion, was not proof. As a matter of law the Crown had not made out to the degree required for their charge of murder. He would *direct* the jury on Monday morning to bring in a verdict of Not Guilty. Meantime the accused would be released, on bail in a nominal sum.

And that is what happened on the Monday morning.

A very, very reluctant jury, by their sullen, obviously bad-tempered foreman, obeyed the judge's clear, plain instructions—it was, he had emphasised, his responsibility, not theirs—and returned a verdict of Not Guilty. Captain Symonds was released. He retired from the Army, married the lady he was living with and (I believe) bought a pub on Dartmoor. He died shortly afterwards.

The Saddest Case I Ever Did

One of many reasons I have for advocating degrees of murder is illustrated by 'the saddest case I ever had'. It was to defend at Maidstone before Mr Justice Chapman a man of good position, high standing and excellent record, on a charge that he had murdered his wife.

'Each man kills the thing he loves', wrote my fellow countryman Oscar Wilde. The couple had had an extremely happy married life together, though not blessed with children. The wife contracted a dreadful incurable disease, which was slow in its progression but very painful. She had begged and begged her husband 'to put her out of her misery'. She had attempted suicide several times. She had written and even broadcast in favour of euthanasia. My client had done everything he possibly could for her. Night and day he had attended to her every need. He was a very nice, very kind, very sensitive man. She was by all accounts a delightful woman.

After months and months of fobbing off her requests to put her out of her misery he one evening yielded. Putting the least possible pressure he could he squeezed her throat—and she died. He immediately telephoned the

police and told them what he had done, saying words to
the effect that his feeling for her was so great that he could
not bear to see her suffering. He was charged with murder.
Our instructing solicitors and I had, I think, three consultations with him. We all liked him enormously. We talked
and talked and talked between ourselves about the case.
There seemed no answer whatsoever to the charge of
murder. We canvassed even 'diminished responsibility' and
had an expert medical witness (I believe my friend and
mainstay, Dr Scott of the Maudsley Hospital) to see him
and prepare a report, but there was of course no question
of 'diminished'.

We determined to plead Not Guilty and try to see
whether judge or jury could find a way out of murder and
its automatic life imprisonment. We do not have degrees
of murder or any such defence as 'mercy killing'—or for
that matter *crime passionelle*.

On the facts—on his own frank statements—he had
known perfectly well what he was doing and intended it,
but *mens rea* did provide just the tiniest of possible pegs.

In the end with the co-operation of a sympathetic prosecution, we pleaded Guilty to manslaughter and I applied,
with more hope than expectation, for an absolute discharge.
And that is what Mr Justice Chapman did. Justice, true
justice, was done.

Lord Havers

Michael Havers, so sadly only briefly lord chancellor
because of ill-health, will always remain attractive in my
memory if only by reason of a case he conducted against
me at St Albans Crown Court when he was attorney general.

I was leading my ex-pupil and close friend Lionel Swift
in defence of a man charged with murder of his wife, on
whom he had inflicted forty-six horrifying stab-wounds.
He was plainly of diminished responsibility. We had strong

medical evidence to that effect, including the very distinguished late Dr Scott of the Maudsley Hospital. The Crown's doctors had come to the same opinion. Our judge was the late Mr Justice Thesiger, who could be a difficult man and on this occasion was particularly so.

When the charge of murder was put to him our client, reading from the formula we had prepared for him, pleaded Not Guilty to murder but Guilty of manslaughter on the ground of diminished responsibility.

Michael Havers got up and said that the Crown accepted that plea.

'Well, I do not', said the judge. 'It seems a plain case of murder to me.'

Michael Havers replied, 'Both Mr Comyn and I have strong medical evidence that it is a case of diminished responsibility.'

'I have doctors, including Dr Scott', I said.

'I know Dr Scott. I've had him before', said the judge disrespectfully. 'As I say, I take the view on the documents before me that it is a plain case of murder.'

I fear I lost my temper then. 'Your Lordship appears to have decided the verdict and consequently the sentence without hearing any evidence at all', I said. 'I would ask that you put the case over to another judge.'

Michael Havers, bless him, got up immediately and said, 'That is an application I fully support.'

The judge looked at us coldly. He then slowly bundled his papers together and pushed them to the side of his desk.

'If that is what you both want', he said, 'that is what you both shall have. Let the case stand over', and to the prison officers, 'Take him away.'

The case subsequently came on before a judge who readily accepted the plea of diminished responsibility and made a hospital order.

I never saw Mr Justice Thesiger but I was reminded of his advice to young women always to carry a pair of protractors when going to the cinema, for use against any would-be assailant.

The Vet

I appeared on one occasion for a veterinary surgeon in Chichester. He was charged with attempting to maim, injure and cause grevious bodily harm to his wife's lover. This by shooting at his private parts from close range.

The weapon used was a vet's instrument of trade—a humane killer.

We decided in consultation to contest the case, on the footing really that the client missed and the the lover deserved a damn good fright—points that could appeal to a jury, however made up.

At the consultation, I impressed all this on the client. 'Whatever you do, don't for goodness' sake ever refer to that instrument as "a humane killer".' He promised.

I got out all the matrimonial details in cross-examination of the lover. He had left his own wife and three young children and set up home with my client's wife and their two young children.

When my client came to give evidence, all went well until he unexpectedly (and at that stage irretrievably) used the words 'humane killer'.

'The instrument you used', I corrected.

'Yes, the humane killer', he said.

I could have humanely killed him.

In cross-examination prosecuting counsel used the offending word twice but otherwise (with unintentional kindness referred to it as exhibit A). The client, *mirabile dictu*, did not use the word at all.

Back in my hands he used it three times in a row. 'Why', I asked him, 'did you use that?' 'The humane killer?' he enjoined. (He was a very stupid man.) 'That's what you call it', I said lightly. 'Oh, everybody calls it that.' he said cheerfully. Then, answering the original question: 'I don't know why really. I suppose it was to frighten him. Because I could have killed him with that, you know.'

Step by step he had shot away our nice little defence. The summing-up was fair. It had to be adverse, and it had to stress that we can't allow *crimes passionelles* in England, or take the law into our own hands.

After a quarter of an hour the jury acquitted. They obviously reckoned that the lover deserved what he so nearly got.

'Well,' said the client cheerfully, 'I obeyed your advice. Could I have exhibit A back?'

Charities

There are two very famous charities—A and B—to which I will never, under any circumstances, subscribe. The reason is because of their conduct in a will case I had.

The deceased was about ninety-five when she died. She left an estate of half a million pounds and two daughters of seventy or thereabouts, who had all their lives been solely dependent upon her.

She had never had any association with or connection with either Charity A or Charity B and had never subscribed to them in her lifetime.

Now by her will, duly executed, she left half her estate to Charity A half to Charity B. The will was not, I need hardly say, drawn by a solicitor, but was on a stationer's printed form. Despite that, it was obviously a valid will.

She made no provision whatever for her two daughters, for whom I was instructed.

Both the charities were obstructive all the way through. At first they offered £15,000 for each daughter. No more. Thirty thousand pounds out of Five Hundred Thousand.

One of our levers was that we would have, or might have, an Inheritance Act claim, but I think the most forceful was our threat to ventilate the whole ugly story in open court. At the court door, they eventually offered, and we took, one hundred thousand pounds for each daughter, plus costs. I still grudge them the remaining three hundred thousand. Charities indeed! Their counsel said to me in the course of negotiations that they had their members to think about, Fiddlesticks! What *really* made them settle at all was my threat—which I meant to carry out to the letter—to open the case 'High' and have them plastered all over the newspapers.

Do you wonder that appeals by these charities—appealing posters, ladies rattling little boxes and all—get no money from me?

Brother and Sister

An old lady left her son her entire £50,000 estate, and her daughter nothing. Other wills had been the other way round. The judge sent us out to try to settle. In the corridor my client said, "After all, she's my flesh and blood as the judge said. I'll be generous and give her £1,000 and costs." "You will not"; I said firmly, "you'll giver her £20,000". He flinched but eventually agreed. The old lady was sane as a sanitary inspector and the will was entirely in order. There was no defence to it—merely 'a merit'. There would equally have been no defence if the will had been the other way round, as it often had been.

So back to the court and we had the judge in.

'I'm happy to say . . .' I said, and I was happy! John Mortimer was happy. The judge was happy. He wreathed himself in smiles. 'Your client', he said, 'has been very well advised. It is a very sensible and just course. I hope it marks a new era in family relationships.'

My client nodded approvingly, generosity written all over his face.

His sister did not smile. Nor did she shake his hand as she left court. I think he really wondered why not.

Enquiry Agents

Divorce is now simple and informal. It certainly was not in my days as a young barrister. Uncontested cases—undefended—had to be strictly proved, before a High Court judge or a special commissioner sitting as a High Court judge. Defended cases were full-blown trials, lasting many days, and often weeks. Adultery was a common ground in both undefendeds and defendeds and very often entailed calling an enquiry agent as to observations kept.

I had numerous quaint and amusing experiences about enquiry agents. One in pursuit of his enquiries crept up at night to the suspect house and put up a ladder to the main bedroom. No sooner had he got up the ladder to the bedroom window than it was slung open by the suspected co-respondent, who promptly tilted ladder (and enquiry agent) away. Both fell to the ground, the unfortunate enquiry agent into a thorn-bush. He had to be treated in hospital.

Another, who tried a more direct approach to a house and was prowling round it on the ground suddenly found the back door burst open and was confronted by the prospective co-respondent, a burly thick-set individual, who promptly laid him out. Ruefully explaining his lack of success to my instructing solicitor later, the agent said, 'I was not aware that he was a former middle-weight boxing champion.'

(Apropos of that I once had a client in an accident case, who laid out the medical examiner for the other side, the insurers. He 'explained' it by saying that he instantly recognised the doctor as one who had examined him in respect of a previous accident and reported adversely on him. The incident did not make this case any easier. I had the mischievousness to ask my opponent whether the doctor had charged any fee on this occasion. Apparently he had.)

There was one enquiry agent who gained entry to a house and the relevant bedroom. The wife in the case reacted by saying 'Young man, have you sense of shame or decency?' He replied, 'Not when I'm on the job.'

Another enquiry agent was deputed to follow a suspected erring husband. He was in luck when he found him at dusk walking along the tow-path of the River Thames in the company of a young woman. The agent was obviously too close and too visible because suddenly the man whipped round, grabbed hold of him and threw him into the river. Having recounted what occurred in his report, the enquiry agent ended with this magnificent observation: 'I think this man suspects he is being followed.'

In one case our side employed an enquiry agent to follow a wife to New York and in New York, where it was suspected that she had a guilty assignment. The cost was naturally heavy. My instructing solicitors were then alarmed to receive a series of cables. The first read: 'Located parties New York. They departing for Chicago. Propose to follow.' Next from Chicago: 'Parties departing Los Angeles. Following.' Then: 'Parties leaving Los Angeles for Mexico. Following.' The expense was by now alarming. I advised countermanding his instructions, but the trouble was that we had no address at which to get hold of the agent. The final message was thankfully: 'They have booked for London and so have I.' No evidence resulted from these vast travels but ironically was readily forthcoming in London. Efforts to beat down the agent's fees were singularly unsuccessful, and the ensuing undefended divorce must have been one of the most costly on record.

Still another enquiry agent was employed to follow a husband from his home in Surrey in the belief that this would lead to his meeting a woman friend. Equipped with an ordinary motor car the agent followed the suspect for a couple of miles but then, as he reported, 'lost him because he was travelling so fast.' Equipping himself with a speedier vehicle the agent tried again but this time lost contact after two and a half miles. He stepped up the power of his car again but this time after three miles lost his potential victim. He next tried a specially tuned car but with the same result. Finally he borrowed a supercharged car and with it managed to keep in touch for four miles. Regretfully reporting all this to the solicitors, he added, 'I have ascertained that this man is a record-holder on the motor-racing track and on water.'

In a case where Cyril Russell briefed me our client had a perfect alibi: she was in a house party two hundred miles away on the night the enquiry agent claimed to have seen her. She had over twenty potential witnesses. The case against her collapsed and the enquiry agent got three years for perjury.

Enquiry agents were not employed only for divorce cases. Their activities cover all sorts of legal proceedings and work wholly unconnected with the law, such as in industry. One I recall in a non-divorce legal case was engaged to keep observation of a plaintiff who was claiming damages for serious personal injuries, alleging amongst other things that as a result of the accident in question he was hardly able to walk. After a couple of observations near the man's home the agent was able proudly to present a film of the plaintiff striding out in the local park exercising his dog.

In accident cases back injuries are the most difficult to deal with. Often doubt and suspicion can be most unfair. On the other hand they can be fairly easily put on. I knew one case which was resolved by an enquiry agent's photographs showing a plaintiff bending down doing his garden.

I have also know enquiry agents usefully employed in detecting illegal trading, exposing fraudulent employees, tracing missing documents, locating witnesses, tracking down 'industrial espionage', and collecting information of all sorts for a variety of purposes.

17

Acting for Lord Lucan and Acting for Private Eye

PRIVATE EYE'S THREE YEAR legal battle with Sir James Goldsmith—christened by their incomparable editor Richard Ingrams 'The Goldenballs Saga'—in fact arose out of a Private Eye article in their issue of 12 December 1975 by the well-known author and journalist Patrick Marnham, part of which dealt with the disappearance of Lord Lucan after the murder—by someone—of his wife's nanny.

It was pure coincidence that I acted for Lord Lucan and subsequently, with Desmond Browne, for *Private Eye*. I acted for Lord Lucan, the seventh earl of Lucan, in the sad, prolonged, contest he had with his wife about their three young children, where he claimed their custody on the ground that his wife was unfit to look after them. This contest which went on during the latter part of 1974 and early part of 1975 was tried by Mr Justice Rees, and Lord Lucan suffered complete and continuous defeat. This he took very badly and he made the most of the access he was given. He made a number of applications and was constantly consulting me about further ones. He was, I can properly say, satisfied for the first time with the nanny his wife had, who was in fact murdered.

She was murdered on the night of 7 November 1975 and immediately afterwards Lord Lucan disappeared and has never been traced since. I in fact saw him in consultation two days before and at that consultation he kindly presented me with a book about the Charge of the Light Brigade, the famous engagement in which an earlier Lord Lucan had taken part. I cannot of course say what took place at the consultation, but it is entirely proper for me to say that he was relatively cheerful and gave no indication of any kind of somebody likely to be involved in the murder of anyone. He was still every worried about his children but as I say it was clear—for once—that he was satisfied with the present nanny.

He disappeared completely just after the murder, but that is very far from saying that he committed it. However, at the inquest (when I did not appear for the Lucan family but Michael Eastham QC—now a High Court judge— splendidly did), the coroner after much deliberation with Michael Eastham summed up to the inquest jury, who brought in a verdict that the nanny was murdered by Lord Lucan

Happily, as the law now is such a specific verdict at an inquest would no longer be possible and it would be for a criminal jury to decide the question if Lord Lucan re-appeared and was tried.

I gather that at Scotland Yard there is a division of view as to whether he is in fact still alive. I have no reason except instinct for saying that I believe he is. He was a tall man of handsome and striking appearance and very pleasant to deal with. He was a whole-time, virtually professional, casino gambler, which always seemed to me a sad thing in a man of undoubted general ability and talent. He never gave any indication in my dealings with him of being in any way a violent man. He was passionate with regard to his children and took loss of them hard, but again it is instinct which makes me feel very strongly that he was not—is not—a murderer. I had no connection with his affairs after that consultation two days before his disap-pearance and my only dealings with the Lucan family were two days afterwards when I had a consultation with them. After that they went to Michael Eastham; who certainly served them well and put up a spirited show for the absent Lord Lucan at the inquest.

The whole Lucan case was a tragedy but a pleasant feature is that by all accounts the children have grown up happy and strong. The eldest son has not assumed the earldom, nor has there been any application to court to presume the death of my client.

An interesting Irish angle of the Lucan case is that the earl had ground-rents from the village of Lucan just outside Dublin and from the town of Castlebar, the position about which is I gather a little chaotic since there is at present no traceable earl!

I came to act for *Private Eye*, Richard Ingrams and Patrick Marnham, through knowing their solicitor, Mr Bindman of Bindman and Partners, for whom I had regularly been acting on behalf of the Race Relations Board since its formation—itself an interesting exercise, which brought us to the House of Lords on a couple of occasions.

The December 1975 article in Issue 465, which caused all the Goldsmith trouble, was only in part references to him in connection with Lord Lucan. It allegedly suggested that Goldsmith aided his disappearance. The second part, which also mentioned him, related to Dominic Elwes and gave the title to the whole article—'All's Well That Ends Elwes'. In regard to that part Goldsmith—perhaps surprisingly— took no action.

Acting for *Private Eye* introduced Desmond Browne and myself to many of their then team; apart from Richard Ingrams and Patrick Marnham, Auberon Waugh, Nigel Dempster, Richard West and Michael Gillard, with all of whom we became on very friendly terms.

Richard Ingrams and Patrick Marnham and Auberon Waugh, with whom we were most closely connected, remain close personal friends. I—and Desmond Browne too—have a very great admiration for them.

Richard Ingrams, the guiding spirit behind *Private Eye* is a very remarkable man—a journalistic genius. *Private Eye* has often been off the rails libellously, but it has always been well able to meet the damages it has had to pay, and their total has been much less than is generally believed. It tends to be forgotten that most newspapers and magazines receive a great number of libel writs every year and in fact settle quite a few of them. *Private Eye* is very reliable on its financial and company information and is compulsory reading in most big financial and business houses. It has a circulation now of more than 200,000—which is far far in excess of the combined total of all the other well-known English magazines.

Richard Ingrams is, it need hardly be said, a man bursting with ideas; a most likeable client and friend. He is not, at any rate at first, very receptive of advice, but he became open to persuasion when he appreciated the advice. It was a pleasure to act for him. His wife, Mary, is also a most delightful person; she runs an attractive bookshop in the Oxfordshire, Thames-side, village of Wallingford. Patrick Marnham is a best-selling author and a leading journalist, now Paris editor for the *Independent*. A very delightful man. Both he and Richard Ingrams have written books about the 'Goldenballs Saga', his going further to be a history of *Private Eye's* first twenty-one years, to 1982, entitled *The Private Eye Story*.

Acting for *Private Eye* involved us in a mass of litigation. Sir James issued over a hundred writs against the paper, its publishers, distributors, retailers and wholesalers and in addition—most serious and worrying of all—a prosecution for criminal libel against the magazine, Richard Ingrams and Patrick Marnham.

I believe that criminal libel is in an unsatisfactory state and in need of urgent reform—a view shared by many lawyers. Not in need of reform is the provision that to prosecute a newspaper for criminal libel one needs the leave of a High Court judge and there is no appeal against either his grant or his refusal of such leave. Here the late Mr Justice Wien gave leave. It ensured his being frequently lampooned thereafter in *Private Eye*. As also, unmercifully, was Lewis Hawser QC, the late Judge Hawser, Senior Official Referee. In my dealings with him throughout the series of proceedings it is right to record him an opponent of whom one could not wish better, fairer or more straight-forward.

The mass of litigation in which Desmond Browne and I found ourselves involved as a result of the one article added up to the following:

8 appearances in the Queen's Bench Division on various matters,
2 of them at Goldsmith's suit for alleged contempt,
2 appearances in the Court of Appeal,
3 appearances in the House of Lords and, finally,
1 appearance at Bow Street Magistrates' Court and then at the Old Bailey.

The civil proceedings never got as far as actual trial of any of the actions; they were all concerned with interlocu-tory, interim matters, such as applications for injunctions and of course two contempt proceedings. I think it would be fair to say that the net result of all of these was really a draw. I say this principally because the main one, an appli-cation by Goldsmith before Mr Justice Donaldson (now Lord Donaldson, Master of the Rolls) for an injunction to restrain the five journalists specified above from writing about him or his solicitor, Eric Levine, pending the criminal libel trial was dismissed by the judge after a long hearing and an appeal against that decision was dropped before the Court of Appeal. Also because two contempt proceedings resulted respectively only in a £1,000 fine and a dismissal respectively. An application by Goldsmith for leave to appeal against the latter was refused by the House of Lords. As against that Goldsmith succeeded in proceedings to proceed for libel against newsagents and we failed in an appeal on that to the Court of Appeal and subsequently in an appli-cation to the House of Lords for leave to appeal.

In one of the contempt proceedings it emerged that private detectives employed by Sir James had been raking through *Private Eye's* dustbin in order to try to find useful information against them. They found some but not a lot.

In a splendid auction which *Private Eye* held to boost
their 'Goldenballs Fund' (a fund which yielded over
£40,000 towards their Goldsmith costs) an excellent cartoon which they published about that went for over
£1,500. It showed three robed judges scavenging in a
large dustbin. There was a cartoon of Lewis Hawser at the
same auction and I said I would buy it as a present for him
if it went reasonably. I had in mind £50 or £60. It went
for £700.

The criminal libel was to me and Desmond Browne the
worrying thing. We thought that there was a distinct risk
of our clients—*Private Eye*, Richard Ingrams and Patrick
Marnham—being found guilty and some risk of a jail
sentence; but more likely a quite hefty fine.

I had many meetings with Lewis Hawser in an effort to
settle the whole lot of proceedings, but they came to
nothing—until just before the criminal proceedings. Then
they and everything were settled, on terms which involved
our clients in full-page newspaper apologies to Sir James
and a very large sum of costs. As part of that settlement
the criminal proceedings were, with the leave of Mr Justice
Bristow, dropped and verdicts of Not Guilty entered. That
was on 16 May 1977.

That criminal proceedings should be 'settled' shocked
Lord Shawcross and he wrote to *The Times* in strong terms
protesting and indeed questioning the ability to do so.

It is interesting to observe that the Director of Public
Prosecutions did not take over the prosecution from Sir
James.

In the committal proceedings at Bow Street I had an
entertaining twenty minutes or so of preliminary cross-
examination of Sir James, in the course of which he quickly
lost his temper with me. We endeavoured there to get the
prosecution thrown out, but that failed as will be obvious
from the subsequent history which I have given.

The settlement was, I think, much encouraged by Fleet
Street—which Sir James had ambitions to enter. He did in

fact subsequently enter it with a paper called 'Now', which failed. The settlement did not prevent incorrigible *Private Eye* from sniping at it, and continuing periodically to snipe at Sir James Goldsmith, but the Old Bailey proved to be the end of all proceedings.

The then editor of the *Sunday Times*, Harold Evans, was a client and friend of mine. He was also a periodic target of *Private Eye* and in acting for them I had to make the most unusual stipulation and reservation—which they readily accepted—that even with regard to them I retained the right to act for Harold Evans. Fortunately their differences with each other never actually led to contested proceedings in court.

I could not, I am afraid, fail to be amused by one of their headlines about him. In a Christmas number a piece about 'Dame Harold Evans', as they liked to call him, was headlined 'Hark the Harold Evans Sing'.

Much of *Private Eye* has always amused me. That is perhaps due to a schoolboy sense of humour and there is much schoolboy humour in *Private Eye*. After all, the idea for it started when Richard Ingrams and others were editing a school magazine at Shrewsbury.

18

Other Cases, and the Bar Council

Spot the Ball

I ENTERED SPOT THE BALL competitions for years (I still do), but the only thing I have won in them is legal fees.

The competitions date from 1936 in the old *Empire News*. Probably the best-known became that in the *News of the World*.

Originally the competition consisted of obliterating the ball in a photograph of a soccer match and requiring competitors by an X to show its original position. But there was a fear that that might be unlawful and the most usual modern method (of many) became requesting competitors to exercise their skill and knowledge as to where the centre of the ball was most likely to be, which would be judged by a panel of experts who, unaware of the ball's location, would choose the most logical spot, which might or might not be the true spot.

Eventually the *News of the World*, for whom I appeared, were prosecuted for their highly successful Spot the Ball, of the modern variety, for alleged contravention of the 1963 Betting, Gaming and Lotteries Act. (There had been a previous Act to similar effect.) It was asserted that the competition was the unlawful forecast of the result of a future event (the panel's adjudication).

The newspaper was found Guilty by the City of London magistrates in September 1971 and fined a total of £50 and costs. An appeal to the High Court was dismissed with costs. We appealed to the House of Lords and I described the competition as being an innocent piece of fun. By a majority of 4–1 the House of Lords in January 1973 allowed the appeal and held the *News of the World's* Spot the Ball to be lawful.

In the leading speech the lord chancellor, Lord Hailsham, said there was no need to give a tortured or extended meaning to the words 'forecast', 'event' or 'result'. He listed the considerations which competitors and panel would take into account (postures of the players, the directions in which they appeared to be looking and moving, etc). In his opinion the competition was not the forecast of a future event (i.e., the panel's decision). There might be cases for prosecution for pure chance or lack of skill but that was not this prosecution.

Lords Reid, Morris and Cross agreed in allowing the appeal. Lord Simon of Glaisdale dissented; he considered that if the competition was lawful Parliament had been cleverly outwitted; in his view the 'future event' was the meeting of the panel, 'the result' their choice and that was 'the forecast'.

Casinos

Over the years I did a number of cases about casinos— applying for licences for them, opposing bids to close them and walking about viewing them, as in the case of the Ritz Hotel, to advise the most advantageous planning from the legal point of view. The vacant basement of the Ritz had great possibilities and has achieved them.

I enjoyed the casino work except for two things. One was the sight of casinos in action afternoon, evening and night, and lots of poker-faced, well-dressed people of both sexes and usually of indeterminate age looking anxiously at a table, and when they lost staying on to try to recoup, until usually at last driven away by losses. I saw many fur-clad elderly ladies betting in units of £100 in—to me—an actually silent, stagnant, dark atmosphere. Eerie!

When Guy Willet and I won a casino at Bournemouth for a well-known hotel there, our clients dined us well at the hotel, made us life members of the casino and gave us tokens to gamble with, mine for £100 and (appropriately for my junior) Guy's for £75. Guy lasted long on his but I was through quickly. I like betting but felt no temptation then, or at any time, to 'buy the table'.

It was on that occasion that a rather embarrassing incident occurred. I decided next morning to have a quick breath of sea air. When I got back, reception were in a terrible state. 'We didn't know you were out', they said, 'and your wife rang from Ireland.' They then told me that they had put the call through to my room and (an Irish) chambermaid had answered it; I rang Anne swiftly and explained everything. It sounded like a very weak case.

I have as counsel been round, I suppose, a dozen or so casinos. There is a great sameness about them. Nearly all provide exceptionally good food services—often, I understand, free to regular patrons. I have had some excellent meals in the course of going to 'a view'—including wine.

The regulations regarding them are very strict and are strictly enforced, but of course there can be no restrictions about money or to 'protect people against themselves'.

I am left with great sympathy for the *habitués* and considerable wonder as to where they got so much money from to bet with. There are of course 'professional gamblers', but *successful* ones of these are few and far between. To me most of the habitués seemed to be playing 'systems'. All I can say is that in my own modest racing I have never found a foolproof 'system', but I must confess that I am not one for 'systems' and have never really stuck at one long enough to give it a good chance.

Casinos have always reminded me of my client Lord Lucan.

The Infallible Test

The presumptuous title to these paragraphs relates to nothing more than how to tell an Irishman from an Englishman. Funnily enough they can sometimes defy distinction. 'I never knew you were Irish', somebody will say. Or, 'I would never have thought you were English.' The infallible test even after years of the national of one island living in the other is to manoevre him or her into pronouncing certain words. Pundits would doubtlessly argue about the words to choose. My choice is as follows.

First the word 'three', and more particularly 'a threepenny stamp or fare'. The Englishman asks for a 'thrupenney', a Irishman for a 'threepinny' or a 'tree-pinny'.

Second the word 'elm'. The Irishman give the 'l' its full force. Likewise the word 'film'.

Next the area of Dublin known as Howth. Only the Irishman, or the knowledgeable Englishman, will pronounce it properly as 'Hoath'. Instances in reverse are Holborn, Reading and Cirencester.

On the point of placenames *emphasis* is often the key. The Irishman speaks of *Man*chester, the Englishman of Man*chester*. The Irishman of *Birm*ingham.

A really good trick, one on emphasis, is regarding 'double words' such as 'post office' or 'post box'. The Irishman calls it 'post *office*', the Englishman '*post* office'. 'Post *box* is to the Englishman '*post* box'. You can indeed use any kind of double-barrelled office for the purpose. It usually works even after years of 'naturalisation'.

'Shur' and 'begorra' are old hat stage-Irish. Try the above or variations.

There are also curious differences of description between Ireland and England. Thus an Irishman speaks of 'tillage', but an Englishman speaks of 'arable land'. An Englishman knows what an 'airing cupboard' is, but would have to think for a moment when his Irish counterpart spoke of a 'hot press'.

I once had a young lady facing me in the witness box who did not realise that I was Irish and for some unaccountable reason did not want herself to be thought Irish. Perhaps it was a time when it was embarrassing to be Irish in England—though I have never found that anything but a matter for pride. Anyway, the accent she adopted was what I can only describe as a mixture of (a) what people think an Oxford accent should be, (b) Rathgar (Dublin suburbs) at its hoity-toitiest and (c) County Cork, from which I think she originally came. I mischievously played my little game and soon 'exposed' her. I then 'accused' her of being as Irish as I was. She 'confessed' with a blush and we then got on to a realistic footing. I think I at least restored her innate pleasure at being Irish.

My Most Embarrassing Moment

Like my friends I have had several embarrassing moments in court, but quite the most embarrassing moment was when I was wearing for the first time a recent Christmas present, a pair of clip-on braces. I was on my feet addressing the Court of Appeal in them, when suddenly 'zing'—one of the back clips gave and hit the back of my neck. Then—and I had suspected it—the other back clip did the same.

I was wearing 'roomy', not tight-fit, trousers at the time and they quickly began to sag. In privacy this might be tolerable but not in the Court of Appeal. I quickly put one hand in my trousers pocket, feeling that this might support them and escape the censure (oral or unspoken) of the court, for courts abhor being addressed by anybody speaking with his hands pocketed.

Alas, one hand did not suffice me. I then put one hand behind my back to grip the trousers. But this made me look and feel like a contortionist and was indeed rather painful. Finally I tried with both hands gripping the front. It felt awful and must have looked awful.

Courts are courteous and helpful when they can be. I accordingly quickly told my junior what had happened and asked if their Lordships 'could give me a few moments'. They must have been surprised, for there was no apparent reason for it, but they said of course they would.

In the corridor my junior reattached the offending clips and since my faith in them had gone he for safety wound a long bookstrap round me.

Thus suspended I returned to court and finished my argument. At the lunch adjournment I begged, borrowed, stole or bought from Tom (Cook) and Charlie (Shepherd) in the robing room a good old fashioned pair of braces. They were a splendid couple and would have made a fortune as comedians on the stage.

Thereafter I used to keep an occasional eye on the buttons themselves to make sure of their durability.

The Witness

It was a custody case concerning two young children and I was appearing for the mother with my former pupil Lionel Swift. Both father and mother were of impeccable character and it was just a question of which could bring up the children best.

The father called a most respectable looking middle-aged man as one of his witnesses as to his suitability. It so happened that we had got quite a lot of material about this witness. I was able to ask him to start with, 'Did you offer your own baby for sale in *The Times*?'

'No', he said urbanely, 'it was in the *Morning Post*.'

'Did you in fact sell him?'

'Yes.'

'For money?'

'Yes, £500.'

The judge was fit to be tied but said nothing, waiting to see what came next.

'Were you an officer in the Royal Navy during the War?'
'Yes'.

This might have rehabilitated him a little with the judge, but I went on: 'Were you cashiered from the Navy?'

'I was.'

'Why was that?'

'I disagreed with the Admiral about certain operations.'

'And made your views public?'

'I did, yes.'

'Do you think you're in a position to judge the fate of the children in this case?'

'I fervently believe the father should have them', he replied.

I sat down soon after that.

The judge gave his judgment and awarded custody to our client, the mother, but said that there was nothing against the father and if anything happened to the mother he would be a suitable custodian.

That night the witness travelled down to Brighton, where the mother lived, and shot her dead.

Arrested for murder (to which he eventually pleaded Guilty) he said that he did so because it would ensure that the father got the children; the judge had said that if anything happened to the mother the father would be a suitable custodian and he felt so strongly on the point that he determined to get rid of the mother.

He was sentenced to the mandatory punishment of life imprisonment.

The Husband

I once appeared for a remarkable husband defending his wife's divorce petition on the ground of cruelty. I advised him that he would not succeed, but he said that he would be divorced on any ground except cruelty—because he had been 'a kind and considerate husband—kindness itself'.

There was, however, no other ground available and he insisted on defending the cruelty.

There were a number of allegations but outstanding among them was that one New Year's Eve, when they were at a bungalow which they had near Windsor, the good husband had thrown his wife and his mother-in-law into the Thames. It was partly this incident that had led me to advise him to let the case go through undefended.

When I called him to answer his wife's charges there was a certain frigidity about the judge. When we came to the New Year's Eve allegation I skipped through it as quickly and largely as possible with a kind of suggestion that it was isolated and regrettable — part of the wear and tear of married life!

The judge intervened strongly. 'Do you mean to stand there, sir', he said, 'and admit that you threw your unfortunate wife and her aged mother into the River Thames on a freezing New Year's Eve?' The agedness of the mother and the freezing of the Thames were touches of the judge's own.

My client was not in the least abashed. 'I know it doesn't sound very good the way your Lordship puts it', he said, 'but if you had to live with them your Lordship would have done exactly the same.'

My advice proved right.

Pascoe

It was ten o'clock on a Saturday night when the jury filed back into the cold, dark and depressing court of the Cornish Assizes at Bodmin. They had been out for over seven hours deciding the fate of my client, Pascoe, and a companion in respect of the killing of a farmer.

The farmer was virtually an hermit, his background being most extraordinary. In the First World War his parents had made a cavern under the house to hide him from being called up for the Forces. He had lived a lonely, isolated life ever since. He had a good deal of money hidden in the house, and this Pascoe knew through having worked for him for a time.

He and his friend decided to rob the farmer, and tied him up very securely. They found no money, and then one or other (each blamed the other) hacked the farmer to death with a knife.

Pascoe emphasised that he had not used the knife at all and that he had protested when his companion, who was in a frenzy, used it.

To convict both there had to be a joint enterprise — for the murder. The trial judge, Mr Justice Thesiger, did not have any doubt about it, but it took the jury an unexpectedly long time to decide.

When they filed back into that eerie and depressing court it was to bring in a verdict of Guilty against both prisoners. Came then the dreadful sentencing to death — at 10 p.m.

The prisoners were removed and my instructing solicitor, my junior and I went to see Pascoe in his cell.

'Tell me, Mr Comyn', he said, ' what's it like being topped?'

I had never heard the word before but immediately knew what it meant — being hanged.

'We won't talk about that now', I said quietly. 'There's still an appeal and a petition to the home secretary and lots of things we can do.'

Alas, they came to nothing and Pascoe was hanged — one of the last to be hanged in England.

The welcome abolition of the death penalty has removed nearly all the strain and all the unhealthy drama and unhealthy public interest in a murder trial.

I often think of Pascoe, a pathetic, semi-literate Cornish lad who lived a gipsy like existence. He was guilty of serious crime certainly, but what if he was telling the truth and had no part in the murder?

He wrote me and the solicitor a short letter of thanks on the day before he was executed.

The Winchester Murder Trial

Guy Willett was a great character on the Western Circuit when I practised on it.

On one occasion I was briefed to lead him at Winchester in defence of an Irishman charged with the murder of a man with whom he was having a row in a bus park near a cinema in Aldershot. There were street hurdles in the concrete park and it was alleged that our client pitched his opponent over one of the hurdles and broke his neck.

I stayed with Guy the night before the case and he 'accused' me of not having sufficient confidence in the defence of my 'fellow countryman'. Guy typically had.

Next morning we went down the cells beneath the dock to see the client. Guy took a chair to illustrate how a running fight could have thrown the victim accidentally over the cross-bar of the hurdle. Unfortunately he went over the top of the chair himself and lay writhing on the hard cell floor.

Our instructing solicitor and I had to carry Guy into court and lay him down on junior counsel's bench amidst moans of agony.

Two things then happened before proceedings began; both in the presence of the jury in waiting. First the judge courteously sympathised about Guy's accident; in reply I thanked the judge and explained Guy's (recumbent) presence in court as being due to his sense of duty. Next the client leant across the deck and in a resounding Irish voice enquired, 'How's poor Mr Willett?'

The case thus got off to a resounding start. I described— but did not illustrate—the 'chair trick' and our client was cleared of both murder and manslaughter. All in all it was Guy Willett's victory. He soon recovered and his crowning comment to me was, 'Look at the lengths I'll go to for a client.'

Chairman of the Bar Council

I was elected vice-chairman of the Bar Council of England and Wales for the year 1973–4 and chairman for the following year. Both entailed a lot of work, the vice-chairman deputising for the chairman at the many meetings and functions which he could not attend. During my year as chairman I was able to do very little practice at the Bar. I understand that it is now intended to pay the chairman a salary.

Our work consisted of dealing with the problems of individual members of the Bar and the problems and interests of the Bar in general. We had to supervise the running of the Bar and represent its multifarious interests on all aspects of practice, making representations to and meeting with authorities who affected them. We were in frequent communication with the courts, the Law Society, the legal aid authorities, ministries, the Lord Chancellor's department and other professional bodies. One day it might be dealing with court administration, the next day with circuit problems, the next with provincial chambers, the next with legal aid, the next with fees and costs and so on. In my time there was a great shortage of chambers accommodation in London and we tried to see what we could do about adjacent premises. Two of the Inns applied for planning permission and I gave evidence in support . In one the Middle Temple applied to have my old chambers, Fountain Court, readapted for use as chambers, and I was much amused to hear counsel opposing it suggest to me that it was 'an architectural gem'.

There were many functions to be attended — lunches, receptions and dinners given by fellow professional organisations and others. I was often at two or three lunches and three of four receptions or dinners during the week. There was much to be gained by friendly co-operation between professional bodies. The Law Society were especially good friends; although we had our differences with them, the field of co-operation was wide.

I visited provincial chambers and kept in touch with the Circuits. I did not go as far abroad as other chairmen have done. There were no international conferences in my time in office. But I went to Luxembourg to visit the EEC Courts and was able to say that I represented two countries of the EEC, England and Ireland. I also visited Paris as a guest of the French Bar, which was most entertaining. I later had the French Battonier over to England as our guest.

When I was vice-chairman I had Roger Parker QC(now Lord Justice Parker) as my chairman, which was very pleasant. With his infinite capacity for hard work he was a very good example. As my vice-chairman and successor I was fortunate to have Patrick Neill QC, now Warden of All Souls. He was particularly kind and helpful when I was ill for a time during my term of office.

My clerk Clement begrudged the time that my chairmanship took me away from practice but regarded it as a great honour and was very skilful in fitting in such cases and consultations as he could.

I had only one point of difference with the Bar Council. I thought there were for too many committees. There was a very substantial majority against my view and I only succeeded in cutting out a couple.

Though not a born administrator or committee-man I enjoyed my two years in office with the Bar Council and besides learning a lot about the inside of my profession hope that I contributed something. Barristers need a strong and forceful Bar Council.

Two Police Officers — and a Third

Two Metropolitan Police officers were up at the Old Bailey before Mr Justice (later Lord Justice) Sebug Shaw for corruption, blackmail, bribery and perversion of the course of justice. My friend David Napley (later Sir David Napley, President of the Law Society) briefed me for Detective

Inspector Robson, and Roger Frisby QC for Sergeant Harris. Another accused police officer had 'skipped his bail' and gone abroad. Detective Chief Superintendent Moody was the officer in charge of the case.

The nature of the charges was dealings with a young man named Perry, extorting money from him under the threat of otherwise framing him with criminal charges. One of the allegations was that Robson smeared his hand with gelignite and held over his head the threat of charging him with possession of it.

It was also alleged against Robson and Harris that they sought information from him as to major criminals and when he did not, or could not, comply extorted money from him under threat of otherwise prosecuting him; further, that they gave him tip-offs about police raids and made him pay for the information.

Perry went to *The Times* with his story and they took it up. They taped telephone calls and meetings and in particular wired-up Perry for one meeting with Robson where it was alleged that he extorted £50 from Perry. This tape was damaging but when produced in court proved to be 'crumpled' at vital places.

The tapes varied in quality and some were difficult to make sense of. The most awkward from our point of view was the one of Robson and the £50, but the 'crumple' occurred at the point when money was alleged to have passed.

Our defence was a complete denial of all charges and that Perry was a young man to whom money was paid, not the other way round.

In the absence of the jury we tried to get the tapes knocked out, first of all on the ground that tapes were inadmissible (there had been very few cases about tapes then). Secondly, on the ground that these tapes were not authentic — that they were not originals but copies and that they had been tampered with . We asked no less than four tape experts to testify to this and the Crown relied on just one expert and *The Times* representatives who organised the tapes.

One of our experts interested me greatly by a graphic example of how easily tapes could be tampered with. He said that if he were given Churchill's war-time speeches he could so cut them and re-arrange them as to produce pro-Nazi speeches. 'This was their finest hour', 'They will never surrender', etc.

The judge rejected our submissions about the tapes and said he would leave the jury to judge their authenticity and value.

When the jury came back and *The Times* representatives gave evidence as to the authenticity of the tapes, they said they were in perfect condition when they handed them over to Scotland Yard and in particular there was no 'crumpling' on the most important tape. It was most disconcerting when one of the jurors, supported by a companion, said that he could decipher the 'crumpled' bit and that it was about the handing over of money.

Perry was a good witness. He was very anti-police, which we did not forget to exploit, and he said that he could mention a number of other corrupt police stations in London. He named one police station in particular as being wholly corrupt.

I cross-examined him and suggested that he was a police informer, which he firmly denied. And I suggested that far from him giving Robson and Harris money they gave him money for information, which he absolutely denied. With regard to the 'crumple' tape he said that on that occasion Robson had demanded £50 from him, which he handed over.

Evidence was given of the other meetings, including photographs, and of the other tapes. To all our answer was that the money which passed was all one way — to Perry as a police informer.

Robson and Harris gave evidence. They were police officers of excellent character and record, with long service.

They put forward the defence I have mentioned and said they had paid large sums of money over a period to Perry.

They were cross-examined by John Mathew.

They were both found Guilty on all counts. Robson was sentenced to seven years and Harris to six. An appeal was unsuccessful.

The third officer mentioned in the title was not the one who absconded but Detective Chief Superintendent Moody, who was in charge of our case. He was subsequently sentenced to twelve years for corruption.

Forging the Prime Minister's Signature —1975

In 1975 I was briefed to appear at Warwick Crown Court before Mr Justice Crichton for a young man named Millhench, who was charged *inter alia* with unlawfully obtaining official No. 10 Downing Street (so headed) notepaper, forging a letter on it purporting to come from Mr Harold Wilson (the then prime minister) and forging Harold Wilson's signature to it.

Leading counsel for the Crown was a splendid man, whom I had only recently come to know but already had come to respect highly and to count as a friend—Harry Skinner QC. He later became a very highly thought of Circuit Court judge in Leicester, where he had been based as a barrister. When personal circumstances allowed, he was quickly promoted to the High Court Bench. It was a great personal, general and judicial sadness that he died very soon after becoming a High Court judge.

My client pleaded Guilty to the forgeries alleged. The Crown accepted his plea and did not proceed with other charges. They all came back to the forgeries in the end.

Harry Skinner, as one would expect, put the prosecution case fully and very fairly. It was my task to make a plea in mitigation. I feared a sentence of about five years; after all, forgery of the Prime Minister's signature on admitted No.

10 Downing Street notepaper was obviously more serious
than many forgeries which came before the courts. I feared
five years. At my most optimistic (and my flocks of geese
often do tend to be swans) I hoped for two years.

There was in fact much to be said in mitigation, starting
with three important points—1) that the forgery of the
name was a very clumsy and easily detected one; 2) that the
contents and phrasing of the letter were equally obviously
ungenuine; and 3) that no real damage had flowed from
it. There were also impressive personal circumstances to
pray in aid. The trouble was that there had been publicity
of what was said in the letter and, as a result of the hearing, there would be wider and worse publicity. I sought to
characterise this latter as being (a) implicit in the very facts
of the forgeries (so that in effect the court should guard
against 'double punishment'), and (b) hopefully, something
of a nine days' wonder.

The Press were of course there in force and had a good
ready-made front-page story. There was no 'sensationalism'
in Harry Skinner's opening of the case for the Crown, and
there was indeed in the event little of any 'sensationalism',
in the worst sense of the word, from the national papers.

I had to be somewhat lengthy in my plea—half to three
quarters of an hour. Mr Justice Chrichton, a most experienced man at the Bar and on the Bench, was everything a
judge should ideally be in such a case (in all cases for that
matter)—courteous, receptive, understanding (if not sym-
pathising) and attentive, showing no sign of impatience.
In short, listening and wanting to get the sentence right.

He did not adjourn to consider sentence. He had of
course had the papers overnight. The Crown had gone 'into
the case fully that morning in court'. So, I hope, had I.

He sentenced the accused to a convenient total of three
years imprisonment—which was generally considered to
be fair, and to be the right sentence. It was certainly a
quite unappealable sentence; one which, interestingly, fell
between my hopes and my fears. My client received it

stoically. He had been a model client throughout—forth-coming with information, receptive of advice and fully appreciating the risk of a really long term of imprisonment. He was most helpful with material for mitigation. He realised, better than almost any client I have had, that mitigation is in truth the hardest task in counsel's reper-toire.Three years meant, with one third remissions for good conduct, two years to freedom. And that is what happened here.

R. v. Will Owen MP

In 1970 I was briefed to defend Will Owen, Labour MP for Morpeth, at the Old Bailey on charges that he had passed secret information to the Czechs in return for payment. Czechoslovakia was then, of course, behind the Iron curtain and allied to Moscow.

I first saw Will Owen in the humiliating surroundings of the interview building at Brixton Prison, where he was in a kind of cage standing with other prisoners waiting for interviews with their lawyers. The building was in a court-yard, which was patrolled by dogs.

We decided to fight the charges. The Crown's case was that as an MP and member of committees of the House he had acquired State secrets and that he sold several of those secrets to the Czechs. In secret session they called a defector who sought to suggest that Will Owen was high up on the list of Czech agents. One starts with certain advantages in cross-examining a self-confessed defector with all that that involves, and I got the feeling that the jury were not very impressed by him.

Will Owen's case was simple if accepted by the jury. He was a leading member of an Anglo-Czech Union; he paid many visits to Czechoslovakia; he was on friendly terms with leading politicians there; he sought to promote Anglo-Czech relations; over the years they had paid him about £2,500 (more than the Crown said) for travel and accommodation. This latter, he said, was quite usual and (this surprised and shocked the jury) several MPs were paid sums to watch certain organisations' interests. He named some of the organisations — mostly trade organisations — but did not name the MPs.

He went on to say that latterly he had begun to feel that the Czechs were seeking to get information out of him.

Foolishly, he did not go to the British authorities and lied to the Czechs. He gave them no secret information but fed them with information which was a mixture of lies and information readily obtainable from reference books.

He was cross-examined for over eight hours but stuck to his guns. There were occasional breaks for him to take tablets for a heart condition. We called character witnesses who gave a very good account of him.

In his summing up Mr Justice (later Lord Justice) John Stephenson said that on his own account Will Owen had 'wobbled on the precipice'; the question was whether he had fallen over.

The jury were out for some hours, then returned with verdicts of Not Guilty on half the counts, the foreman indicating that they could not agree on the remainder.

Told by the judge to try, they retired again and within three quarters of an hour were back with verdicts of Not Guilty on the remainder.

So Will Owen was completely acquitted.

On my advice he had resigned his seat early on. He wrote to me later that he was in poor health and in poor financial circumstances. He died a few years later in his mid-sixties, leaving a widow but no children.

Peter Rawlinson, long time attorney general—who should have been lord chancellor—prosecuted me in other spy cases but not in *Owen*. In his elegant book *A Price Too High* he says that Will Owen, when 'safe from further prosecution', spoke freely to the Security Service about his dealings with

Czech Intelligence. Well, he was acquitted after a long and careful trial and eight hours cross-examination.

Hong Kong

I twice applied to be admitted to the Inner Bar in Ireland but was twice refused by the Irish Government—so unlike my welcome in Gibraltar and Hong Kong, where on producing my certificates of call to the English and Irish Bars (I in fact only needed one) I was immediately called to the Inner Bar and following on that was admitted as QC.

I think I may have been the pioneer from these islands to the Gibraltar Bar. They were certainly unused to any visiting barrister. The case was all about the early stages of a libel action and we sensibly settled the whole case.

I am reasonably certain that I *was* the pioneer to Hong Kong. Now, over twenty years later, there are members of the English Bar there all the time. I christened it the Far Eastern Circuit.

There were Irishmen and Englishmen in official positions there; for example, Sir Michael Hogan, Chief Justice. Judges then were usually from the western world.

I had two summonses to Hong Kong, on separate cases. The first was to get the Court of Appeal if possible to give our nice Chinese client a larger lump sum against her ex-husband. I think we were seeking a million and a half Hong Kong dollars. I found out that divorce was a stigma for a woman in the Chinese community.

Her father was a very wealthy man, who owned a hotel and generously asked my wife, my clerk (Clement) and the managing clerk of London solicitors who were involved (George Parry) to be his guests—giving my wife and myself in addition first-class return tickets.

A nice touch was that Clement and George Parry found a cheap charter flight from Amsterdam with the 'Australian Friends of Ireland'.

We arrived about a day after Clement. We found him waiting for us at customs, ready to pilot us through as if he had been there for years. He had thoughtfully obtained for me a set of summer robes. The case lasted seven days and during that time, enterprising as ever, he fixed me consultations in two other cases from other clients.

We received considerable hospitality from our hotelier host and from our instructing solicitor, Donald Cheung and his wife. His brother, Ossie Cheung QC, was leader for the opposition in our case.

We were also splendidly entertained by members of the Bar, Chinese, Anglo-Chinese, native-born and settlers. We learnt from them such customs as the shame of 'losing face' and the unpropitious nature of certain days for doing certain things; for example, one local barrister would not allow Anne and myself to enter a certain building by the front door because 'the omens' were against it.

We were shown around Hong Kong by our new-found friends. On the golf course there were numerous graves and little tablets commemorating ancestors. The golf course was near the Chinese border and we heard with surprise that many essential commodities, such as milk and water, came from China. Reflection reminded us that Hong Kong, so heavily built up, could not possibly supply milk for its five million inhabitants.

Kowloon is the large mainland part of Hong Kong. It contains every known type of shopping, but what appalled us was to see hotels and grand buildings in the main streets but behind them, a matter of yards, shacks consisting of sheds and large boxes with whole families—also dogs and hens—squalidly occupying them. Here there were open drains which we saw people using. Hong Kong was certainly a place of contrasts—richness and opulence alongside dreadful poverty.

Haggling was expected in the shops, even the main shops. I had an experience of local commerce when I bought some ivories and wood carvings. I was a few dol-

lars short of the finally agreed price. I told the sales lady
and she just said, 'Gimme all you got.' It summed up local
dealing for me in a very graphic way.

At Mass on Sunday we expected a Chinese priest but
what surprised us—and, of course, should not have been a
surprise at all—was that the figures in the stations, including the Virgin and Christ, bore yellow faces. Mass was
conducted and the sermon given in Cantonese, the most
used Chinese dialect.

After all this it was desirable to win the case—as we did,
with one of the three judges dissenting. The client used
the lump sum to buy and furnish a house in a London
suburb. She told me that there was no future in Hong
Kong society for a divorcée—even though she was the
innocent party.

There was great celebration at the hotel that night; my
client kindly gave me a nice-looking Swiss watch. Some
time later I had to get it repaired in Dublin and was very
surprised to hear the watchmaker say, 'I expect you know,
but this is a very, very valuable watch.'

Anne and I flew back by scheduled air plane. Clement
and Mr Parry attached themselves again to some tour
which left them back at Amsterdam.

The runway at Hong Kong ended at the edge of the
sea—which I must say I found a little disquieting both on
arrival and on departure. For that matter, landing or taking off at Gibraltar exercises the mind because there is that
Rock in the way.

My second trip to Hong Kong was about nine months
later—alone. I had that rare thing, an unlosable case. It
really was unlosable. My client, a well known Hong Kong
surgeon, had been sued by a lady for breach of promise.
But the promise had been made while he was already
married and that made it unenforceable at law.

We had a consultation soon after I arrived (I think
Ronnie Arculli was again my junior). I had already given a

written opinion but now explained the legal position to the client orally. He was extremely worried and said that he could not possibly fight the case, because of the publicity. I said I thought I could stifle a lot of the publicity by making a carefully worded preliminary objection. But no; he said that he must settle, whatever the cost. The local solicitor and I tried and tried to persuade him to fight. At worst the case could be dealt with shortly and without him giving evidence. The solicitor pointed out that people would quickly get to know about the case even if it was settled.

However, in the end we had to act on our client's adamant instructions. We opened negotiations.

The lady's price was high. I think she started at a million Hong Kong dollars and we beat her down to three-quarters of a million. In return I insisted that she should hand over to my instructing solicitor every communication she had had from our client. As far as I know she faithfully kept her promise on that. She of course got her costs. So the unlosable case was lost—with costs.

On this occasion I stayed at the same hotel, the one owned by my former client's father. He gave me a great welcome and absolutely refused to charge me. But expecting to be there for a week I was London-bound after a couple of days. I had done the Case of the Insistent Surgeon.

Defending Denning

The splendid Lord Denning, Master of the Rolls, often did not see eye to eye with the House of Lords. Whose was the better eye is often discussed and in many instances remains to be seen.

The story is told that on one occasion counsel in the House of Lords was taking three points against a judgment of Lord Denning when after about five minutes a tug hooted on the river which flows past their Lordships.

As the tug hooted, one of their Lordships remarked, 'Well, that disposes of Lord Denning's first point.'

In another case Lord Hailsham said that a finding of Lord Denning was 'fortified by the authority of a quotation from *Hymns Ancient and Modern*.'

If one took a count I suspect one would find that Lord Denning was as much reproved by the House of Lords as approved by them. Their language got stronger and stronger but he didn't mind a bit.

In one of my last cases before becoming a judge I had the task of defending Lord Denning before the House of Lords. We won, he won, but only after the House of Lords had given him a monumental ticking-off.

The case was *Davis v. Johnson*, where under the Domestic Violence Act my client, Miss Davis, sought to exclude her partner Johnson from the house they both owned equally. Two divisions of the Court of Appeal in previous cases had held they had no power to grant an injunction. Lord Denning convened a full court of five and with disdain for precedent led Miss Davis to a 3–2 victory. The dissenting two held that they were bound by the precedent of the two earlier court of Appeal sessions.

Mr Johnson took the matter to the Lords, where a lot of time was spent 'telling off' Lord Denning for departing from the Court of Appeal's duty to follow precedent (which incidentally the House of Lords had freed themselves from doing).

Argument as to the law and facts of the case was rather an anti-climax after this precedent palaver, but Miss Davis (and Lord Denning) won comfortably. It seemed to me rather like a scorer of the winning goal being sent off the field.

My father

When he retired from the Irish Bar—a senior counsel and Father of the Munster Circuit—my father came to live with me in London during term-time. We returned to Belvin for vacations.

In London he spent most of his time at the Law Courts and the Old Bailey, following my cases. He did not come on circuit with me on the Western Circuit which I loved and enjoyed as much as he did the Munster Circuit.

Then one day when the court rose for lunch Clement came up to me and said, 'I have some bad news for you. Your father is in Charing Cross Hospital with a suspected fractured skull. It appears he fell down the steps into the Central Hall.'

The diagnosis of a fractured skull was correct. He was unconsious for over a month. The hospital could not have been nicer or better.

He recovered, up to a point. I was the only person he really recognised. He often thought he was back in Ireland, and on the Munster Circuit.

He died a couple of years later. A wonderful father.

Remembered

I had four very pleasant days doing an Agricultural Holdings Act case in the Isle of Wight. All the farmer in me came out as we jeeped and walked the two hundred and fifty acres of which my client, the landlord, was claiming possession on the ground of bad husbandry. Belvin's farming shortcomings were very much in my mind as we examined with disgust broken gates, dilapidated fencing and overgrown hedges. 'Tut', we said to ourselves, 'tut', my 'tut' being *sotto voce*.

The case came on next day and we lasted the rest of the week, the unfortunate tenant getting knocked at every turn. I spent about twenty minutes cross-examining him about weeds alone. We made the place sound like a complete shambles.

We duly won and after some refreshment the landlord and my instructing solicitor saw me ferrying off to London.

I heard nothing from the solicitors until ten years later—yes, ten years. They rang up my clerk, Clement. 'We remember Mr Comyn,' they said; 'we have a big civil case and are looking for counsel.' Then came the punch-line. 'Does Mr Comyn do anything apart from Agricultural Holdings Act work?'

'What did you say, Clement?' I asked.

With a twinkle in his eye Clement replied, 'I said "Oh yes, sometimes." It's overseas work and I have arranged fees accordingly.'

A similar incident occurred when I was sitting for the first and only time as a local elections officer. It was at Mold in North Wales. Everybody was wanting to unseat everybody for the most shocking electoral abuses. Then, in mid-afternoon, quite, quite suddenly it all collapsed—settled. I asked the four young counsel into my room for tea. Over tea one said to me charmingly, 'Do you ever get bored with this electoral work, sir, sitting day in, day out?' 'Do you?' I asked, and there was no reply.

Discipline

I have I think appeared before most of the professional disciplinary bodies. My career in that field started just after the war, before a tribunal called the Egg Disciplinary Board, or words to that effect (it has been long since abolished). My client was charged with selling stale eggs (duck) and stale eggs (hen).

After a long battle (with expert witnesses involved!) I submitted No Case in regard to the eggs (hen), and the charge was dismissed. But after a further tussle we went down on eggs (duck). It seemed a bit harsh but our man was prohibited from keeping ducks for six months. 'Not to worry', my cheerful solicitor said to him, 'try geese and turkeys.' The disconsolate client kept saying, 'My poor, poor ducks.'

It was perhaps fitting that my last case at the Bar should be a disciplinary matter. It was to defend with Robin Simpson QC for *the fourth time* before the Bar Disciplinary Council a certain well-known QC. The previous charges were rudeness to a judge, not telling the truth to a judge and being at Ascot races when he should have been in court. The summary is tame compared to the details. On those first three occasions we somehow or other (I don't quite know how) managed to keep our client practising. But on the fourth occasion (misbehaviour to a judge and leaving a case suddenly, with his junior hardly able to speak English) he was suspended from practice for a year.

We appealed. Such an appeal went to a panel of judges called 'The Visitors'. Now the trial judge had in his turn not behaved very well and had said some unfortunate things. This I think more than anything else persuaded the three appeal judges to allow the appeal and lift the suspension.

Lord Merriman

Lord Merriman, President of the Probate, Divorce and Admiralty Division as it then was (now the Family Division), was a most remarkable character. My experiences before him with and without E.H.P. would fill a book by themselves.

He sat with another judge on a divisional court. One day I got up and said, 'This is an appeal from the Kingston-upon-Thames justices.' 'Now that's a coincidence,' said the President; 'we had an appeal this morning from the Kingston-upon-Hull justices.' He then told me about that case.

On another occasion I told him that the justices had deliberately disregarded a judgment of his Lordship. 'Ho, ho,' he said, 'we'll see about that. We can't have justices going off on a frolic of their own, can we, Mr Comyn?'

'Give me the headlines,' was a favourite phrase of his. Once I said, 'With respect, my Lord, I can give it all in one headline. Derby Justices Wrong about Adultery.'

'Splendid,' he said, 'we'll explore this adultery after lunch!'

Knowing him so well I didn't often make tactical mistakes before him. One when I did was after hearing him in the case before describe the justices' notes as 'woefully inadequate' and throw them about on his desk. When I got up for my case I waved a single piece of paper about and said, 'These cases seem to go in cycles, my Lord. Here is another with a woefully inadequate Note.' The President took the Note, which was shorter than the one in the previous case. Having read it he said slowly, 'My Comyn, Mr Comyn, it is a model of compression— only a few nails maybe but every one of them a nail in your coffin.'

One morning in rather a bad temper after reading a Court of Appeal decision in *The Times*, he suddenly said to me, whose case was three or four away, 'Mr Comyn, is what I say of less importance than what the Court of Appeal says?'

I thought hard and quickly. 'That surely can't be so, my Lord, when you are a member of the highest tribunals in the land, the House of Lords and the Privy Council.' His face wreathed in smiles. 'D'ye know, I'd forgotten that. Thank you very much indeed, Mr Comyn. I'm most grateful.'

Forgotten it? Only six months before in the Privy Council he had expressly approved a decision of his own, saying words to the effect, 'One cannot improve upon words of my own in *A v. A.*'

Once in a case about cruelty called *Simpson v. Simspon* Roger Ormrod was acting and was tied up for the morning, so Clement put me in to cover. Roger's and his estimate was just over half a day, so I might have to finish it. With the President it lasted fifteen days. Roger Ormrod, Robin Dunn and I 'boxed and coxed' to keep it covered.

One last Presidential incident for the present. E.H.P. was leading me in a defended cruelty. He must for a rarity have been snoozing because he suddenly rose to his feet and said, 'I don't know if your Lordship got that. The witness has just said "Headington".' 'Yes, indeed, but I'll still write it down.' As he was writing it down the unfortunate witness said, 'I never said "Headington", I said "Teddington".'

'Now then, sir', said my Lord, 'don't try and trifle with me. I heard you and leading counsel heard you quite distinctly.'

'I don't even know where Headington is,' persisted the witness. 'Teddington, yes. We live there.'

'Don't be ridiculous. Headington is in Oxford, where I was privileged to be educated.'

'I've never been there, sir.'

'Now if you go on like this I know what to do with you.'

A quarter of an hour of this followed and the witness, who was entirely right, was never the same again.

'Are you calling me a liar?' enquired the President.

'Yes—I mean no, no, no.'

19

On the Bench

On Being a Judge

I REFUSED THE FIRST OFFER of a High Court judge-ship, from Lord Chancellor Hailsham, but about three years later accepted the renewed offer from Lord Chancellor Elwyn-Jones.

I was conscious that accepting a judgeship meant giving up life at the Bar with all its excitements and interests, and its companionship—giving it up for a new life, which I did not know I would be suitable for or suited to.

In the event I had ten years as a judge, when I had to retire because of ill-health. I had one year in the Family Division and the remainder in the Queen's Bench Division.

I enjoyed my time as a judge but nothing like as much as my time as a QC. The work was not so hard but was obviously more responsible. There was humour and good fellowship between the judges—when they met. But one's colleagues of the Bar were largely cut off and the congenial life of chambers was gone. It was on the whole a lonely and responsible life.

I had had some criminal judicial experience as a recorder—first of Andover, when boroughs had their own recorders, and then after 1972 as a recorder at large on the Western Circuit when the new Crown Court system was introduced. A recordership is a part-time judicial appointment.

The Crown Court sits in three tiers—High Court judge, Circuit Court judge and recorder, according to the degrees of gravity involved in the case. On one occasion, a counsel told me later, his case had been listed on Monday and Tuesday before the High Court judge but not reached; then on Wednesday and Thursday before the Circuit judge and not reached; and was then put in on Friday before me as recorder. 'Gor', said the client, 'I've been demoted to the ruddy third division.'

The only civil matters I had tried before going to the Bench were occasionally as an arbitrator and two weeks as a deputy High Court judge in the Queen's Bench Division. I confess I never liked the idea of deputy judges.

I had also been a Commission of Assize on the Western Circuit.

I did not like being in the Family Division. Although I had done a lot of work there when I was at the Bar, it was very different having to decide cases as distinct from argue them. I found children cases particularly worrying, and there were a great number of them, dealing with custody, care and control and access. The parents were mostly at loggerheads. It was sad to see such unreasonableness in people who had once been happy together and who had, together, brought these children into the world.

I did not care much either for disputes between divorced parties on all manner of things, principally finance and property. Not so many ex-husbands were as evasive about their means as ex-wives alleged. And ex-wives could be equally untruthful about their means of support.

I remember one man who swore that he had no assets of any kind. The mansion he occupied was owned by one company, the two Rolls-Royces and an aeroplane which he used were owned by another company, a yacht by a third company and, believe it or not, a prize Jersey herd by yet another company. For money he relied upon 'petty cash' drawings from several other companies which he 'owned'. I was not long in unscrambling his companies and giving the ex-wife a lump sum and proper maintenance. To his protests I replied that he could easily find the money.

In the ordinary run of cases it often occurred to me to wonder how an average man could afford to re-marry and in effect run two homes. The second marriage must labour under the strain of maintenance for the first marriage, and I imagine there must be a certain amount of resentment by the second wife. If there are children by both marriages, the strain must be almost unbearable.

Freddie White

My old friend and client Freddie White of Collyer-Bristow and Company used to seek to reassure me about sitting in the Family Division, where he had given me so much work. He used to come into my court quite often, and standing just inside the door would give me a friendly smile. On a few occasions, he passed me light-hearted notes pulling my leg.

I will never forgive Freddie for giving me a brief for the day of the Varsity rugger match—and then going off to Twickenham himself. But I suppose, in turn, he will not forgive me for going off with his overcoat (plus season ticket etc.) on a wet November night.

I am told that in one of his cases I was perhaps being too placid and complacent. He said to my junior, 'Get James to lose his temper and we'll win this case.' I did— and we won.

I applied to be transferred to the Queen's Bench Division and thankfully was. I was at my happiest trying crime and civil. I sat in the Law Courts, at the Old Bailey and on Circuit at many of the cities and towns in the country. Circuit was homely as we lived in special lodgings and did not often leave them between coming back from court at about 5 p.m. until next morning.

At Cardiff there was an amusing incident later recounted to me by counsel. There were three judges sitting—a

Welshman, an Englishman and myself. A man up for a
criminal offence asked counsel whether it would be possible to have 'the Irish bloke' to try him. He was, I gather,
very disappointed when put in before his fellow-Welshman.

I did not much care for the panoply of Circuit; police
escorts, police outriders and police (sometimes patrol dogs
too) in the grounds of lodgings. It always amused me that
one was seen off at the local station with great pomp and
circumstance but one's arrival at London with one's clerk
meant having to queue for a taxi.

It was interesting sitting at the old Bailey, where I had
appeared so often. No. 1 Court particularly (which I called
the Centre Court).

I tried all manner of crime at the Old Bailey. Two cases
in particular stand out. One was the trial of a man described
as 'a super-super grass'. He had given the police names
and details of dozens of crimes, including murder. He was
up for double murder himself and for other offences. He
pleaded Guilty, but both prosecution and defence were
anxious to stress his great co-operation, no doubt to lead
to early parole on his mandatory life sentence for murder
and to try to get as lenient as possible sentences in respect
of the other offences. I felt I had to stress that grasses,
whether super or super-super, could not automatically
expect reduced sentences, but here, bearing in mind the
mandatory life sentences for murder, I was able to pass
four-year sentences for the other offences.

So that the accused could not be seen by the public,
wooden shutters were placed around the deck.

I saw shortly afterwards that the first person charged
with murder on this man's information was acquitted.

The other case was in 1980 for criminal libel, where a
Mr Gleaves, self-styled Bishop of Chatham, of 'the Old
Roman Catholic Church', brought a private prosecution
against Mr Deakin and a colleague as authors of a book
that said Gleaves was a menace to boys and young men
and had committed offences against them. After a week's

hearing the jury found the accused Not Guilty, the alleged libels being true and published in the public interest. After the trial the attorney general intervened to stop legal proceedings by Mr Gleaves.

The law of criminal libel in England is in a very unsatisfactory state. There has, amongst other things, been a lot of confusion between civil and criminal libel and about the ingredients of criminal libel. In *Gleaves v. Deakin* I defined criminal libel for the jury as being 'a written statement so serious in itself, and so greatly affecting a person's character and reputation, as to justify invoking criminal law and punishment instead of, or as well as, the civil law and damages.'

I tried a great number of civil cases, many of them running down actions and claims by workmen. One of the most unfortunate of the latter class was where a workman coming out of one room stumbled into and right across another and with his shoulder or elbow set in motion machinery which was unfenced because it was not in use. He lost a hand as a result. I felt constrained to dismiss the claim, regarding it as a pure accident, a chance in a million, that there should have been such a combination of circumstances.

In a case where a tour bus overturned and injured a wife and husband, the latter very seriously, I awarded the wife damages for her own personal shock and, breaking new ground, for the shock which she suffered as a result of her husband's injuries, separately.

In a case which I called 'The Case of the Company's Cuff-Links' I found in a wife's claim against her husband's company that several items of jewellery and decoration did not in fact belong to the company at all but were hers; and they included the cuff-links.

There were two medical negligence cases tried together, relating to operations on a woman's throat, the second surgeon having been consulted after the first. I had strong views about the negligence of both surgeons and favoured the plaintiff against each of them. There was no appeal on

behalf of the second. But the first went to the Court of
Appeal and won 2–1. The case then went to the House
of Lords and he won 5–nil. With great respect I felt that
the majority judges did not pay sufficient regard to a
trial judge seeing and hearing the witnesses and seemed
to elevate a doctor's position far beyond the proper duty
of care.

The Moonies Case

Way back in 1962 I was counsel in the longest divorce
case ever heard in England—*Boyd Gibbons v. Boyd Gibbons,
Roman and Halperin*. It lasted for twenty-eight days
before Mr Justice Lloyd Jones and resulted in my client,
the husband, getting a decree on the ground of his wife's
adultery with the second co-respondent, John Halperin.

Now in 1980–81 I was to preside as judge over the
longest and costliest defamation action there has ever been,
Orme v. Associated Newspapers Ltd (the *Daily Mail*). It
lasted from 6 October 1980 until 31 March 1981. Eleven
jurors out of the original twelve survived the course.

The case arose in this way. Sun Myung Moon, variously
called the Reverend Moon and Dr Moon, was a South
Korean living in the United States, who had founded a
body called the Unification Church, otherwise The Holy
Spirit Association for the Unification of World Christianity.
He gave it the role of a church, was himself cast as the
Messiah and laid down its tenets in various publications
and pronouncements. Included in the ceremonial were
mass marriages conducted by him between partners he
chose for each other. Exceptionally one Irish girl objected
to the partner chosen for her and the Reverend Moon
then substituted someone else.

The followers of the Reverend Moon—and there were
many—were inevitably called Moonies and his organisation
called the Moonies.

The Moonies were a prosperous and widespread organisation. They recruited as members people of all ages but principally personable young people in their twenties of good background and education. Many of these they used to collect funds on the streets and in public places.

Their recruitment and their fund-raising were very successful, but joining involved severing connection with one's family. So imbued did young people become with the organisation that few left, and those who remained were dedicated to it.

The main scene of activity was California but there was a flourishing branch in England under the English director, Mr Denis Orme. He was the effective plaintiff in the legal proceedings, although there was another plaintiff, who took no active part.

The proceedings, for libel, arose because of an article in the *Daily Mail* two and half years before, castigating the Moonies; under the headline 'THE CHURCH THAT BREAKS UP FAMILIES' it described it as a 'sinister' organisation and suggested that it was not a church at all but a commercial undertaking which seduced, brainwashed and exploited young people. It gave two stories of young people, one English and one American.

Mr Orme sued as head of the Moonies in England. He had not been mentioned at all in the article but there had been a photograph of the Moonies' headquarters in Lancaster Gate in London, where he lived and which he ran. I ruled that accordingly the words were capable of referring to him.

The *Daily Mail* in their defence pleaded justification (truth) and fair comment.

At the trial Mr Orme was represented by Geoffrey Shaw and the *Daily Mail* by Lord Rawlinson QC, Richard Rampton and Edward Garnier. I have never known a case done better on either side.

The plaintiff called seventy-six witnesses and the defence over thirty. Mr Orme gave evidence at length and was

rigorously cross-examined by Lord Rawlinson, who brought
him through all the features and characteristics of the
Moonies. It transpired that they had charitable status in
England and two trust funds.

Throughout the trial Lord Rawlinson sought the atten-
dance of the Reverend Moon, but to no avail. He was so
persistent about this that I eventually said I would only
allow him to mention it every other Tuesday morning!

The parade of witnesses included, for the plaintiff,
happy and contented adherents who had cheerfully given
up everything for the Moonies; for the defendants the witnesses included parents of broken homes and disillusioned
members of the organisation. There were in addition a
considerable number of documents.

After counsel's speeches I summed up to the jury com-
paratively shortly. My summing-up took just over a day. I
believe that a summing-up should be as brief and simple as
possible. In a case such as this I cut through the techni-
calities, tried to classify the central issues and summarised the
evidence quite shortly. I finished summing-up shortly after
3 p.m. and the jury retired, going to a hotel for the night.

The jury returned to court shortly after the luncheon
adjournment next day with their verdict. They found for
the defendants, the *Daily Mail.* They asked to bring in two
riders. I am always cautious about riders because goodness knows what they are going to be. However, I let the
foreman of this jury read out the riders. The first was that
the jury urged that 'the tax status of the Unification Church
be investigated by the Inland Revenue on the grounds
that it is a political organisation.' (As I understand, it continues to retain its charitable status.) The second rider was
that the jury expressed their 'deep compassion for the
young idealistic members of the organisation'.

It was accordingly judgment for the defendants, and I
made an order for costs in their favour. They were absolutely
ensured of a substantial sum by reason of orders I had
made during the trial for the plaintiff to put up substantial

sums by way of security for costs, which orders were unsuc-
cessfully appealed to the Court of Appeal during the trial.

In a mammoth trial such as this, one's greatest fear is
a disagreement by the jury and the prospect of a re-trial.
It is dreadful to contemplate. But evidently there was no
danger of disagreement with this jury.

A Difficult Wardship

The most difficult case I ever tried was a wardship matter
concerning little Peter, aged eleven and a half.

Both his parents were killed in a car crash. His brother
George aged thirteen went to their grandparents, their
father's parents, who were in their middle fifties and in
good health. For some reason Peter went into the care of
local authority, the grandparents protesting.

Without going to the court the local authority placed
Peter with a young couple Mr and Mrs X with a view to
adoption, and he had been with them getting on for six
months and was well and happy with them. Now the
grandparents on one side and Mr and Mrs X on the other
both sought care and control of young Peter.

I was impressed by both sides. I saw the great advantage of Peter joining George with their grandparents. I
also saw the wrench it would be to remove him from a
new home he had found with loving and caring young
people, whom he was just beginning to look upon as a
new father and mother.

The interests of the child being paramount, I had to try
to overlook the heartbreak of each side if the matter went
against them.

I agonised about the case and for once noticeably lost
sleep about a case.

I eventually decided to give Peter to his grandparents,
where he would be in the family and with his brother
George. He had been put with Mr and Mrs X without the

authority of the court and therefore wrongly. The passage of time was unfortunate, the inevitable heartbreak of Mr and Mrs X was very sad, but I thought that the interest of the child was that he should be with his grandparents and his brother, so close in age to him and with whom he had been on excellent terms.

How would you decide?

I gave a stay pending appeal and there was an appeal. The Court of Appeal unanimously held that I was wrong and left Peter with Mr and Mrs X and (this I found surprising) gave regular access to the grandparents and brother.

Jameson v. the BBC

This was a case which I tried with a jury in 1984 and it had an unusual and happy ending.

Derek Jameson, former editor of the *Daily Star* and the *Daily Express* and the *News of the World*, and former managing editor of the *Daily Mirror*, sued the BBC for libel in respect of a Radio 4 'week ending' programme which described him as 'an East End boy makes bad' who had turned the *Express* 'into the thinking men's bin liner' with a policy of 'all the nudes fit to print and all the news printed to fit'. It said that he had a pre-occupation with nudes.

The BBC defended the action and were represented by an old friend and opponent of mine, John Wilmers QC, whose premature death has been a great loss to the Bar. The BBC's line was that what they said in a satirical programme was true and/or fair comment. John Wilmers epitomised it by saying that a former editor should have a thick skin and be able to take criticism as well as give it.

Whatever the merits of the case I found Mr Jameson in his long time in the witness box a very likeable and pleasant person. I was at pains to point out to him and the jury that there was nothing to be ashamed of in having come from the East End and that it should rather be a matter of pride. In an entertaining book he has written he describes me as having been very quiet and having hardly said a word. My wife's comment was that if that was really true I must have been ill or sickening for something!

I confess that I expected a verdict for Mr Jameson with a moderate sum of damages. But the jury bought in a verdict for the BBC, so there was judgment for them with costs.

The happy ending? The BBC employed Mr Jameson regularly and he has done some excellent programmes for them.

I forget whether I mentioned at the outset of the trial that I had once been employed by the BBC! I rather think I did and that no one objected to my trying the case!

A feature of the case which I thought unfortunate was counsel insisting upon a number of questions for the jury. I prefer where possible, 'How do you find—for the plaintiff or the defendant? If for the plaintiff, how much?'

'Tea Ladies'

One case I tried became known to the press as 'The Tea Lady's Case' or 'The Teapot Case', or (as one paper said) 'A Real Storm in a Teacup').

Coffee 'breaks' and tea 'breaks' have long been a part of English (and Irish) factory and office life. At the Bar I used unashamedly to take every opportunity which was legitimately offered to have his Lordship rise 'for a few moments' mid-morning so that I, my junior and our instructing solicitor, could have 'a quick coffee'—and I two or three Sweet Aftons—in the coffee room of the crypt in the Law Courts in London. That charming and erudite Chancery judge, Mr Justice Goulding, I only got to know towards the end of my career at the Bar, shortly before I became a judge. It was the Advocaat Case. He later told me that I had brought the coffee/cigarette 'break' into Chancery tradition !

Now apparently in industrial and office life a lot of time used to be wasted by coffee and tea 'breaks', so the idea grew up of having 'a tea lady' moving along with a trolley and serving employees at their benches or office desks or tables.

One such lady, employed by a famous company, injured her hand quite seriously through, as she said, lifting too heavy a teapot to pour out tea. She sued her employers in negligence, alleging that she had previously drawn the attention of her manager to the hazard involved and to the fact that she had already shown signs of injury; but nothing was done.

The company, through their insurers, contested the claim. They put in issue the claims of undue heaviness and prior complaint and said that anyway this could not found a case against them. For one thing it was all a quite ordinary and usual task, with nothing hazardous about it. Two, she knew the situation perfectly well. And three, there were steps she could have readily taken to ease any strain from pouring out tea from a heavy pot.

I believed the lady's evidence—that the teapot was too heavy for her and that she had complained about it. In fairness the manager agreed that she had once said something about it, but not (he said) in any way amounting to a complaint, more a comment.

Counsel and I did 'experiments' with the teapot in question in open court, and at home in the evening I 'experimented' with teapots of various sizes.

I found in her favour. I said that 'tea-ladies' were an important part of modern life and that the teapot in question was very heavy indeed when full and too heavy and awkward for her to manage. I believed that she had made what amounted to a complaint and a warning and that she had suffered real, though not too serious, injury. Sufficient to incapacitate her as a 'tea-lady'. I consequently found the defendants negligent and awarded her damages and costs.

'An Englishman's Home'

A sad case I had where I dearly wanted 'to strain the law'—where even Lord Denning could not strain it—was where a retired colonel of about seventy-two, a widower with no children, came before me in person on a 'judicial review'. He appeared for himself but had the support of two old army contemporaries. He complained that having saved up to buy himself on retirement a country retreat in Kent near a river (fishing was his great hobby) he had suddenly and unexpectedly received a compulsory acquisition order forfeiting his property, on the ground that it was required in order to drive a main road through it.

He was of course opposed by the appropriate ministry. They were represented by Treasury counsel, John Laws, a counsel whom I always very greatly admired.

The retired colonel simply said to me, 'My Lord—can they do this? To me—a veteran of two World Wars? Is not an Englishman's Home his Castle?'

I was, I confess, very upset, very moved. Perhaps that was a tendency and a fault of mine as a judge. Judges should, I feel, care but ideally, when they have decided something, put it behind them.

John Laws explained the position, clearly—and kindly. As kindly as his instructions allowed.

I tried everything I could to get the ministry in question to do something to help the retired colonel. Could they not, I asked, slightly re-route the road? Through, say, some nearby agricultural land?

No. Their experts had spoken. They were implacable.

I searched with all my accumulated knowledge of years to find some defect or flaw in the ministry's case, in the ministry's notice. I could find none.

I was minded, very minded, to quash the notice and let the ministry appeal—which of course they would do, and with inevitable success. But my duty was to administer the law, however unfair I thought it was. So I had to tell the retired colonel that an Englishman's Home was no longer his Castle—if High Authority wanted it. He was absolutely baffled. So were his veteran friends. Between them they had received an accumulation of high military decorations of two wars.

I felt absolutely awful. No doubt it was in the over-all public interest to have this wretched road and to have it straight through the retired colonel's garden and drawing-room. But would it not have been possible to put it a half mile or so to the right or left?

A judge has to remember his oath—to administer the law, whatever he may privately think. So I had to, simply had to, dismiss the retired colonel's application.

He appealed to the Court of Appeal. They told him, kindly and with regret, that he had no case and his appeal against my decision had to be dismissed.

I feel, as strongly as I can possibly say, that sometimes (I do not say that this was such a case) bureaucracy is not as attentive to, as sympathetic to, as appreciative of, the individual as it might be.

20

Varia

Lord Goddard on a Judgment He Had Just Pronounced

I WAS BRIEFED TO APPEAR for a plaintiff in a running down, personal injuries, case at Winchester Assizes before Lord Goddard, the then Lord Chief Justice.

It was not a particularly serious case. If the plaintiff, a charming middle aged married lady of about fifty-five, from rural Hampshire, won, she could expect to get about £10,000, to include her special damage (actual expenses).

However, the defendant's insurance company were denying liability for the accident which had caused her injuries (and her expenses), and liability had its difficulties for us.

They had paid into court the sum of £5,000.

I advised the client to take it and told her that though she was out of time for taking it out of court and thus getting her costs up to date of payment in, I reckoned that I could by negotiation with my opponent get her her costs up to date; I could, I said, perhaps even get her another £250 or £500.

'No, thank you', she said, 'I want to fight the case.'

So we did. She was an excellent witness, and difficult though the case was I thought we had just about won. Not so. In a typically short, typically definite, not gruff (he reserved gruffness for criminal cases) judgment, the Lord Chief Justice found against us, all along the line.

My opponent asked for judgment for the defendant.

'Yes.'

'And payment out to the defendant's solicitors of £5,000 and accrued interest, my Lord'.

Lord Goddard looked at me.

'Good God Almighty', he said, 'Is there money in court?'.

'Yes, my Lord', I said ruefully.

'Well, it's quite clear my judgment is entirely wrong,' said that truly Great man. 'You must appeal at once, Mr Comyn'.

We did—and settled the case for £7,000.

I had Lord Goddard's granddaughter, Katie Sachs, as a pupil. He was properly tougher towards me then. One day after leaving his court Katie said to me, 'Wasn't Grandpa sweet?' It wasn't the apt word in that particular case. She it was who was sweet, and the pity is that she did not continue at the Law.

The View

It was an accident case at assizes. The plaintiff workman was suing his employer for injuries sustained when loading cattle off a loading bank. The loading bank was, he alleged, unsafe. Counsel for the plaintiff got a very rough time from the judge all through the day. The judge was inclined to the view, as he said more than once, that the plaintiff surely had eyes in his head. In the late afternoon the plaintiff's counsel suggested, wearily but firmly, that it might be a good idea if his Lordship had a view of the *locus in quo*. The judge did not like the suggestion a bit (he felt it would be intolerable if a judge had to view the scene of everything), but eventually he consented, observing that justice must not only be done but be seen to be done. It is a remark which does not always bear itself out.

Cars were laid on and the party travelled twelve miles to the scene of the accident. His Lordship travelled in his full robes. It rained throughout most of the journey, which did not improve things. The judge's clerk clutched the large umbrella (almost a golf umbrella) which he had brought, and cursed the prospect of having to squelch around holding it over the judge. But the rain stopped just as they were arriving at the place.

The judge was athletic (he had been a well-known sprinter in his university days) and he sprang out of the car and up the loading bank in an instant, leaving the two counsel and the rest of the party far behind. Unhappily the rain had made the bank particularly slippery. More unhappily still there were holes in the bank, made no doubt by the hooves of cattle. His Lordship caught his foot in one such hole, slipped and was thrown down the other side of the bank, where he came to rest in a pool of water which had collected there and which was not very clean either. Nothing was said. The judge was assisted to his feet, he was cleaned up a bit and the party returned— in silence—to the court. There the case was adjourned until next morning.

Counsel for the defendant should have thought of settling the case, but he would not do so. Next morning when addressing the judge he ventured to recall some of the judge's observations of the previous day—that the plain-tiff, after all, had eyes in his head.

The judge wasn't having that.

'Quite so', he said, 'but he'd have needed eyes in the back of his head to avoid a death-trap like that.'

Perjury

Perjury is rife. When you come to think of it, there are over 200 courts of all kinds sitting in England and Wales every day and in contested cases one or other of the parties must usually be committing perjury. But there are very few prosecutions for this everyday perjury, because of difficulty of criminal proof and the fact that the accused would maintain that he had been telling the truth and was wrongly disbelieved by the other court.

At Carlisle Crown Court I had a strange will case before Mr Justice Hollings against one of my old colleagues, Owen Stable QC, now a Circuit judge. We were setting up a will and the other side were contending that the testator's signature was a forgery. We had strong evidence, particularly two attesting witnesses. One who was particularly impressive gave excellent evidence on a Friday but on the Monday morning decided to end his evidence. Having received permission to talk to him I then had no option but to abandon our case. The judge, against my urgings, sent the papers to the Director of Public Prosecutions and the witness was prosecuted for perjury. He pleaded guilty and got three years.

Owen Stable and his side were generous to us in defeat and, proving the earlier will which they set up, agreed to pay us some money and something towards our costs.

Owen was a son of that famous character, Mr Justice 'Owlie' Stable, who had a knack of achieving justice even by unorthodox means. He once said to me when I was defending a Pakistani for murder, 'Mr Comyn, the Appeal Court wouldn't approve of this, but if you plead Guilty to manslaughter I'll be lenient.' He was, too.

Owen Stable dressed impeccably but unusually, particularly wearing a bow tie with his winged collar and special spongey uncreased trousers of greyish colour. He was once described as looking like the racing correspondent of the *Church Times*.

He was forever pulling my leg and did so unmercifully during the will case at Carlisle. I got part of my own back when he produced his own gold watch and chain in court to illustrate a point and I asked that they should be made an exhibit.

I encountered another curious perjury case when I was sitting in the Court of Criminal Appeal with Lord Lane,

Lord Chief Justice. It was an appeal by a woman police constable against a sentence of fifteen months imprisonment. She admitted to falsifying a parking offence by saying that a car was in a restricted place when it was in fact elsewhere. This was apparently so inexplicable that we felt there must be something more to it, something behind it. We kept pressing her counsel for an explanation but he maintained that she could not (? would not) give one. It was useless to speculate and in the absence of explanation we dismissed the appeal. My theory was that she was acting for some police officer friend who for some reason of his own wanted this false charge brought against the motorist.

The Cardiff Councillors' Case

I had seven weeks in Cardiff before Mr Justice Paull defending an alderman in a conspiracy prosecution alleging that he and three fellow councillors (also accused) had corruptly given his son—a solicitor (also accused)— planning permission in respect of a certain valuable site. In brief, the main defence was that the planning committee had no idea that the son was the applicant, because the application was in the name of a company and there was nothing to indicate that the son was involved.

In one of those ways that happen, the prosecution case began to crack. Progressively the three councillors and the son were discharged. But my submission of No Case to Answer was rejected, and I had to call my client. I also called a character witness, an ex-Welsh rugby international— which helped!

Then the judge started to sum up and something happened which is unique in my experience: the foreman of the jury got up after about twenty minutes of summing up and asked the judge if they could bring in a verdict of Not Guilty there and then if they had heard enough. The judge was obviously taken aback by this novelty but after a moment's thought agreed, and my client was triumphantly acquitted.

The judge pulled my leg afterwards by saying that he reckoned I had managed to make five pleas of No Case. I said I thought I was only three.

We got our costs. Shortly afterwards the client sought some refund of the fees he had paid me—but my splendid clerk Clement was not one to make refunds, so nothing came of that.

Brian Jones of the Rolling Stones

In the early 1960s, when use of cannabis was less frequent and prosecutions about it too, I appeared at London sessions before Reginald (Reggie) Seaton on cannabis charges for a delightful and famous character, Brian Jones (now alas dead), the guitarist of the Rolling Stones. He was also, funnily enough, their negotiator with the BBC.

We had no possible defence to the cannabis charges (which did not include pushing) and he pleaded guilty to them. In mitigation I said that Brian Jones had assured me that he was finished with drugs and wanted his followers and the youth of the country to heed his present plight and the mess drugs had made of his life. All along I thought the penalty would be a hefty fine, but Reggie Seaton (turning my points against me) said that the accused was an idol of youth throughout the country and should have given a proper example to them, and sent him to prison for nine months.

Our immediate application for bail pending appeal was refused, but next day we got bail from a High Court judge.

On the morning when the appeal was on in the Court of Criminal Appeal, just as I was getting ready to go over to court, I got an hysterical telephone call from Brian Jones from a call-box, at Wimbledon. He said he could not face it. I sternly told him that if he did not come he would be quickly picked up and lodged in prison. One night of it had already had a profound effect on him. He was to get a taxi to the Law Courts immediately. We got on well together. He obeyed me. He arrived, and the court was packed to bursting with fans and members of his and other groups. With the leave of the court we called a famous psychiatrist, Dr Neustatter. He thought Jones could give up drugs and was fundamentally a sound and good young man. Courts—and in particular the Court of Criminal Appeal—always respected what Dr Neustatter said. Quite apart from his eminence, it was well known that he would not give evidence in 'any old case' but only in one which he had faith in. His evidence more than anything else persuaded the CCA to give Brian Jones 'another chance' and to substitute a fine of £1,000 for an imprisonment.

A Denning

I often appeared before that unique judge, Lord Denning, Master of the Rolls. It was always a pleasant if somewhat unexpected experience. Once I was before him as appellant and opened my case by saying, 'I appear for a poor widow of eighty-seven who has been ejected from her little flat by order of the county council.'

"Cum, now, Mr Cummyn,' said Lord Denning, 'we are a court of law, you know, not a court of sympathy.'

There was a moment's pause and then he said, 'What age did you say this poor old widow was?'

21

Belvin

BELVIN, TARA, HAS BEEN MY MAIN home since I was about eight, when Aunty D acquired it, and she left it to me when she died. I subsequently added about a hundred and fifty acres to the forty which it possessed. It is a lovely Georgian house in County Meath, some twenty-five miles form Dublin and near the Hill of Tara.

It is perhaps apt that Meath, a county which suffered much at the hands of Cromwell, should be known as the 'Royal County', but the description is not due to any past or recent association with English royalty. It simply refers to the fact that the ancient kings of Ireland had their seat at Tara—the Tara of 'The Harp that Once'. From the Hill of Tara, 512 feet above sea level, there is a most wonderful view, ranging from the mountains of Ulster in the North to the hills of Wicklow in the South and from the sea on the East right across the central plain of Ireland. One can picture the kings from their height keeping a watchful eye on all that was going on around and below.

Meath is a county embracing probably the greatest source of historic interest in Ireland—from pagan days to Christianity and thereafter right up to the time of the famous, much-recalled, over-remembered, Battle of the Boyne in 1690.

Tara's fame covers the period from about 4000 BC to about AD 500 and during that period it was the cultural and political capital of the country. A national assembly was held there at intervals where problems were discussed, laws promulgated and law cases decided. There was indeed a legal court similar to the much later Court of

Crown Cases Reserved, to which difficult cases were reserved for decision. Festivals of great splendour were also
held yearly. 'The Five Roads of Tara', radiating to all parts
of the country, were thronged on these great occasions.

The visitor may be surprised and a little disappointed
that it is not a place of ruins readily visible but of earthen
mounds. These, however, are very impressive and of great
archaeological interest. The most striking are various hill
forts. The Royal Enclosure (an oval about 950 feet by
800 feet, surrounded by a wide fosse), Cormac's House,
the Mound of the Hostages, the Rath of the Synods and
the Banqueting Hall. The remains of the latter consist of
two parallel banks about 750 feet long between which is a
long sunken area about ninety feet broad. Entertainments
there were obviously on a lavish scale and one ancient
account speaks of 'thrice fifty steaming cooks!'

In AD 433 St Patrick met the then high king, Laoghaire,
at Tara, and with the coming of Christianity the glory
of Tara began to wane. Ancient prophecy that it would
become as deserted as it had been populated came—and
remains—true.

Linked with Tara were the burial place at Dowth and
Newgrange, the latter being reckoned one of the finest
burial cairns in Europe.

With Christianity came the spread of monasticism and
Meath is rich in its relics of early and late monastic
settlements. Monasterboice goes back to the sixth century.
Its most famous 'ruins' are a round tower and two high
crosses elaborately decorated with religious scenes and in
an excellent state of preservation. The round tower is a
feature of Ireland and owes its origin to the raids by Danes
and Norsemen in the ninth, tenth and eleventh centuries.
The monks built these towers for the dual purpose of
providing a place of refuge and a watch tower at the same
time. The rounded shape of the towers made for easier
construction and also had the advantage that raiders could
not remove stones from the base. The entrance was

usually several feet above the ground and access was gained by means of a ladder which was hauled up quickly after use.

When looking at the round towers and castles of Ireland I irresistibly conjure up pictures of besieged inhabitants pouring boiling oil over their assailants and of chefs working overtime down below to provide it. 'My compliments to the chef and could he make it just a little thicker and a little hotter.'

Meath is the constant envy of other counties for its splendid grazing land, which must rank as among the best in Europe. A drive through the county also shows herds of magnificent beef cattle, and famous stud farms.

The original Belvin was built in about 1700. Parts date at least five centuries earlier. The trees on the avenue and the numerous turnings discourage unwelcome callers. They did not, however, deter those who chose to burn it in 1981—presumably one of the subversive organisations. Only the fabric and the thick walls prevented it being a total loss. We rebuilt it just as it was.

On the side of the house is a small building which is at least 600 years old and has interesting stone carvings depicting the Garden of Eden. Certain of the out-buildings are probably as old.

In the adjoining orchard garden are two medium-sized beeches which were cleverly trained into each other to form an attractive arch—a natural frame for family photographs. Also in the orchard, a good two hundred yards from the house, is an odd little stone building, divided in two by a stone wall and with a door on either side. Dilapidated now, it is possible to see that at each side within there is a very deep hole. It is the remains of an old outdoor lavatory. Whatever for, you may well ask? Well, you don't suppose, do you, that a house like Belvin in the old days permitted its servants lavatorial facilities under its own roof? Rain or fine, day or night, the unfortunate domestics had in necessity—presumably sometimes in dire necessity—to brave it to the outside lavatory, and back. It was, I believe, called the Relieving Office.

Belvin itself has had a curious lavatorial history. Within my own knowledge it has had no less than three successive indoor lavatories. The first two were only artificially speaking 'inside lavatories'. They jutted out into the main yard, resting on iron pillars. The first suddenly developed an alarming gap from the house when my father was actually using it; *in situ*. He jumped rapidly to safety and it lurched out drunkenly, to be finally taken down by contractors. They adopted the same system for reinstatement—with the same end result. Good sense finally prevailed to put the third lavatory truly inside the house.

With regard to water, until recently we had to rely on a well in the yard. It goes down over 300 feet and I much regret the contract I made with the diviner for a charge of £1 per foot. We now have Council water as well.

It fell to us to bring electricity and the telephone to Belvin. The Telephone Department charged me something like £2 a pole to carry the phone from its nearest point, the local shop over a mile away. I bear a friendly resentment that they now carry a number of lines on from me, without payment.

Installing the electricity provided a number of incidents. It dispensed with the oil lamps and candles and I missed particularly the Aladdin lamps which had to be pumped and gave such a splendid light. But far and away the most exciting and frightening feature was when I was lying on the drawingroom sofa and thought the chandelier a little out of true. So it proved to be. We found that the electricians we employed had hooked the chandelier from the floor above by a butcher's skewer, which had slipped.

The telephone was originally a pleasant toy. It was manual and the charming local postmistress, Mrs Manley, was able to tell callers when we were out and often where we were. In earlier days her husband delivered telegrams by hand. The refreshment provided to him by my father varied with whether the contents contained good news or bad.

The Forestry Commission, a splendid body, once wrote
to me to say that their representative was sorry that I was
away when he called to inspect but that he had received
every assistance from my 'head forester'. For a time I feared
a request for a substantial rise from our solitary workman,
Mick Allen!

I plant thousands of trees myself each year and have
very promising plantations. My rate of loss is low but my
fault is planting too closely. When planting young trees
one should allow for space—what they will be like when
fully grown. Rabbits and hares are the main enemies of my
young trees, biting the tops and if necessary going on
tiptoes to do so. Copper beech and oak are surprisingly
quick growers there.

We specialise in beef cattle and I have a small pedigree
herd of Aberdeen Angus, which has been pleasantly successful. I know a lot about shows and may one day write a
book called *There's no business like show business*. One story
in it will be of the man who carried a tin of Black Nugget
polish to eliminate areas of this black breed which were
going white or grey. Another will be of the owner who
had plainly falsified the date of birth in a young bull class.
His entry dwarfed its rivals and had to be declared the
winner. A runner-up from Northern Ireland said to me,
'Meath land is certainly wonderful. It can put months on a
calf.'

I was helped in showing by two friends, Michael Martin
and John East. The latter appeared on television at least
three times from Dublin shows, speaking on such di-
verse subjects as the standard of entries and what went
into mating and preparing a bull like 'our' Victor, three
times champion at Dublin! Michael Martin was an equal
'character'. He was a painter and decorator. On one
occasion when he was painting a church a trestle board
slipped and decapitated the saints on the epistle side.
Michael stuck the heads back but was never sure that he
got them right.

In the days when we could afford and had a steward at Belvin, he and Michael Martin took a dislike to each other. One day when the steward was away, Michael turned up at his cottage with a bowl and spoon, castor sugar and cream and ate six rows of strawberries which the steward had planted, plucking the remaining six rows and taking them home with him.

He was very proud to be photographed holding Victor and to lead him in the prize-winner's parade. On one occasion when I led him myself, he stood on my big toe with all his ton plus and I was lame for weeks.

I left marriage late, until I was forty-six. I married Anne Chaundler, a solicitor. In the old days of segregation of the professions, this would probably have meant my being disbarred and she struck off the rolls, especially as we met professionally! She used to brief me. Her father and grandfather were solicitors in Biggleswade in Bedfordshire. We have two children, Rory and Kate, and our main home is at Belvin. We were married in my local church by the parish priest, Father Cooney, and the reception was at Belvin, organised by Michael Martin.

Anne did splendid work in restoring the old Belvin and then after the bombing in organising the building of the new Belvin, exactly as it was.

Father Cooney was a great friend of ours until his death. On one occasion he was sitting in the study at Belvin with me and observed two storage heaters, part of a number which I had in fact bought from him when he installed oil heaters in the church. 'Whatever possessed you, James', he said 'to get storage heaters? I once had some in the chapel but they were perfectly useless. I was frightfully lucky to get rid of them.' I smiled and just said, 'Who bought them?' 'Do you know', he replied, 'I can't remember. All I can remember is how glad I was to get rid of them, useless things.'

22

Light Verse

I have spoken earlier of my hobby of writing light verses. Here are a few examples.

The River of Goodness

See the sober River Liffey
Saunter on in solemn state
Through the pleasant lands of Wicklow
Till it gets to James's Gate.

See it then, agush with Guinness,
Stagger forward on its way
Till it passes out completely
When it gets to Dublin Bay.

The Hive

A thousand bees in a hive together
Came a day that was nice and warm,
'Now', said one, 'there's a change in the weather,
Don't you think that we ought to swarm?'

Murmurs came of a Drone's dissension,
'I suggest that we'd better not;
Agreed the weather is as you mention
But isn't it really much too hot?'

The Leprechaun

I know a little leprechaun
Who enters for the Pools,
He's streets ahead in pixie-craft
Of permutating schools.
He picks his teams for Saturday,
This little Irish elf,
Then visits them invisibly
And plays for them himself.

The Absentee Landlord

The Absentee Landlord in Ireland
Always seemed to the people a curse,
But to live with your landlord in England
Can often be very much worse.

Epitaph on a Steeplechaser
(previously published in the *Spectator*)

You ran through my money, if ran be the word,
And now 'neath this turf you are safely interred,
In Elysian Fields you now practise your tricks,
What a change it must be to get over the Styx.

Epitaph on Leading Counsel

The mortal remains of a leader rest
In the silent depth of this lonely tomb,
In life he was usually heard at his best
At four o'clock in the Robing Room.

We Needn't Trouble You

Observe your opponent perspiring,
Resuming his kicked-upon seat,
An air of all gloom and depression,
The picture of abject defeat.

But do not be too much elated.
Let sympathy lavish in lieu.
Remember you might have been called on—
Remember it might have been you.

Oh Lady Fair

Oh Lady fair
With the golden hair,
May I try
To get liberty to apply?

The Dutiful Son

For a dutiful son it is sad to relate
That I only got costs from my father's estate.

The Optimist

An optimist who's next to none
Is he whose rival's holed in one
And says without a smile or laugh,
'I've now got this one for a half.'

The Film Star

I know a pretty lady
Who features on the screen.
And constant litigation
Is part of her routine.
She never briefs a leader,
She doesn't see the need,
For throughout the whole proceedings
She always plays the lead.

The New Appointment

Rumoured in the Robing Room,
Tipped throughout the Crypt,
His clerks were over-cautious
And waited till they knew—
Then couldn't get their money on
At more than 5 to 2.

For a Silver Wedding

Take all the silver memories you've gathered by the way
And add to them the blessings that crowd on you today,
Take all of these together and so be gently led
Across the silver river to golden years ahead.

Modernity

In days before restrictions,
There was something different there,
A gem of Architecture
A glorious Georgian square.
But now in place of beauty
These horrid boxes stand,
A monument to show that
We're town and country planned.

The Stockbroker's Letter

We'd surely stick if we were you
To what you hold in Scottish Glue,
For recently there's been a hum
That they will merge with Ghana Gum,
Who then in turn we think have hopes
Of tie-ups with United Ropes.
And if in fact these firms combine
They'll surely threaten Threaded Twine,
Who'll find themselves so awkward placed
They'll have to bid for Standard Paste,
Who as you know have got control
Of most (well, virtually the whole)
Of Plaster and Adhesive Tape,
The leading binders in The Cape.
So certainly the thing to do
Is not to part with Scottish Glue,
Especially since they've replied
That all the rumours are denied.

Wicklow

As I work in the heart of the city
I indulge in my favourite dream,
A cottage away in the mountain,
By the edge of a Wicklow stream.

I think of the forest beside me
Of the larch and the fir and the pine.
In all there is only an acre,
But the whole of that acre is mine.